Lee, Weston
Torrent in the desert

DATE DUE

Torrent in the Desert

Navajo Mountain

Color Photographs & Text
by Weston & Jeanne Lee

Endpapers & Maps
by Don Perceval

 NORTHLAND PRESS

Flagstaff, Arizona

Mcmlxii

Torrent in the Desert

To the River
*— its might, beauty
and wilderness*

foreword

The Colorado River of western North America is unique among the great rivers of the world, whose basins for the most part contain the centers of early civilizations. The Yangtze and Huang Ho of China, the Ganges and the Indus of the Indian Peninsula, the Tigris-Euphrates, Nile, Danube, and Mississippi valleys are recognized as the centers of early high culture. Not so the mighty Colorado, which for about eighty percent of its length flows in deep canyons. Where the canyons are absent, high altitudes or scorching desert climate make farming difficult or impossible on much of its flood plain. Today vast stretches of the Colorado basin are completely uninhabited.

The distinctive assets of the Colorado River and its tributaries are their scenic beauty, their scientific and historic features, and their recreational potential, which have begun to be appreciated only in recent years. Cardenas, one of Coronado's lieutenants, who first discovered the Grand Canyon, thought little of the beauty and viewed the area as useless from the practical standpoint; later explorers cursed the sheer-walled cliffs, the deep canyons and the rugged terrain for the problems these presented, or avoided the Colorado completely. Very limited sections of the river were used for transportation, and then only with great difficulty.

In the last fifty years the preservation of great scenic areas in the United States has come under the National Park Service. A trend even more far-reaching and one that is drastically changing the native qualities of our rivers is man's development of dams, irrigation and water-storage projects, and power production. Only through control of the Colorado's waters by dams of increasing size and number has the river been tamed so that its potential productive value can be utilized.

Man's desire to change the face of the earth for his benefit will forever deface large areas of magnificent wilderness. Arguments rage today between the advocates of water-storage and power projects for the Colorado and those who want its natural beauty preserved. Under the pressure of today's population needs, the conservationists have lost many large sections of the river.

Realizing the trend, Weston and Jeanne Lee spent their vacations and weekends studying and photographing the Colorado and its tributaries from the headwaters to the Gulf of California Their book shows the Colorado as it has been during recent years, prior to completion of the currently authorized dams.

The Lees' pictures and text tell the story of the River. This is not their story, but that of the Colorado—the last that can be written of this great, unique drainage system. Future generations will not be able to see for themselves large segments of what has been portrayed here. The lovely tributaries of Glen Canyon will soon be gone; other dams under construction and proposed will create lakes where canyons and valleys now contain the stream and its associated life-complex, distinct from that of any other river. All who love the Colorado, or who will wonder what it was like, are fortunate in having this record.

Edward B. Danson
*Director, Museum
of Northern Arizona*

Acknowledgments

The authors are grateful to the many individuals and organizations who have given help and encouragement in a challenging task.

We are indebted to the United States Geological Survey, the Bureau of Reclamation, and the National Park Service, without whose public information services our field work would have been impossible. We appreciate the responsiveness of these agencies and the courtesy of their staffs.

We are indebted also the Museum of Northern Arizona and the Utah State Historical Society, where we were welcomed to the archives and permitted to quote freely from publications.

The cooperation and seasoned experience of the Harris-Brennan River Expeditions, Canyon Tours, Inc., and "Moqui" Mac Ellingson greatly facilitated the water-level phase of our canyon photography.

To Mrs. Suzanne Colton Wilson of Tucson, Arizona, and Mr. Paul E. Weaver, Jr. of Flagstaff go our special thanks, for it was their enthusiasm and confidence which brought this project to its fulfillment.

Weston and Jeanne Lee

Contents

I *A Mountain Stream Comes of Age* 1

II *From the Rooftops of the Continent* 57

III *Down the Plateau Province* 101

Introduction

Among the multitude of rivers which lace the slopes of North America, one stands alone in awesome grandeur. No other can match it—for the depth of its plunge from headwaters in the high Rockies to the Gulf of California—for the bewildering variety of climate and terrain through which it passes—for the immeasurable power of its falling waters, now meandering as a pasture creek, now thundering between great cliffs of basalt or pausing in its descent to form a vast many-forked lake amid the desert ranges. This river is our Colorado.

A story of the Colorado properly begins as a tale of two rivers, much alike in nature and flowing to a common end, but gathering their water from sources far apart on the western slopes of the Continental Divide. Into these two rivers and their tributaries drain the streams of our great Southwest country, with its treasure of natural wealth, and in part they give the answer to Daniel Webster's query of another century: "What do we want of that vast and worthless area, that region of savages and wild beasts, of shifting sands and whirling wind, of dust, of cactus and prairie dogs? To what use could we ever hope to put those great deserts and those endless mountain ranges . . .?"

In the northern regions of the towering Colorado Rockies rises the branch known to early trappers and explorers as the

"Grand", a name which has been given to many localities in its watershed. The Grand, now called the Upper Colorado, carves a 400-mile channel southwestward through the mountains and broken tablelands of western Colorado state and eastern Utah to its confluence with the Green River in the remote fastness of our deep canyon land.

The more northerly branch of the Colorado heads among the eternal snows of the Wind River range in west central Wyoming. From the glacier-born lakes where it is formed, the Green flows south and west through the foothills of the Divide into a great arid basin, then enters a kaleidoscopic series of gorges in its passage through the Uinta uplands. Continuing southward among the plateaus and intervening valleys of east central Utah, this dynamic tributary reaches its rendezvous with the Grand, in a supremely dramatic setting.

The Colorado River, born of this union, makes its way for more than a thousand miles to the sea as it drains an area where horizontal-lying sedimentary rock layers have been elevated en masse, broken into great tilted blocks, sharply folded and in places eroded away to their granite foundations, punctured by volcanic intrusions, and etched in a deep multi-branching pattern by tributary streams—descending finally through rugged desert ranges of ancient heat-fused rock onto a vast alluvial plain which ends in the tidal morass of the river's estuary.

These pages are designed for those who would seek the Colorado in its many roles—explore its origin in the continental highlands, follow it through broad alcove and seething chasm, marvel at the perpetual sculpture of the Grand Canyon—and for all who revere the wild and the beautiful.

Chapter 1

A Mountain Stream Comes of Age

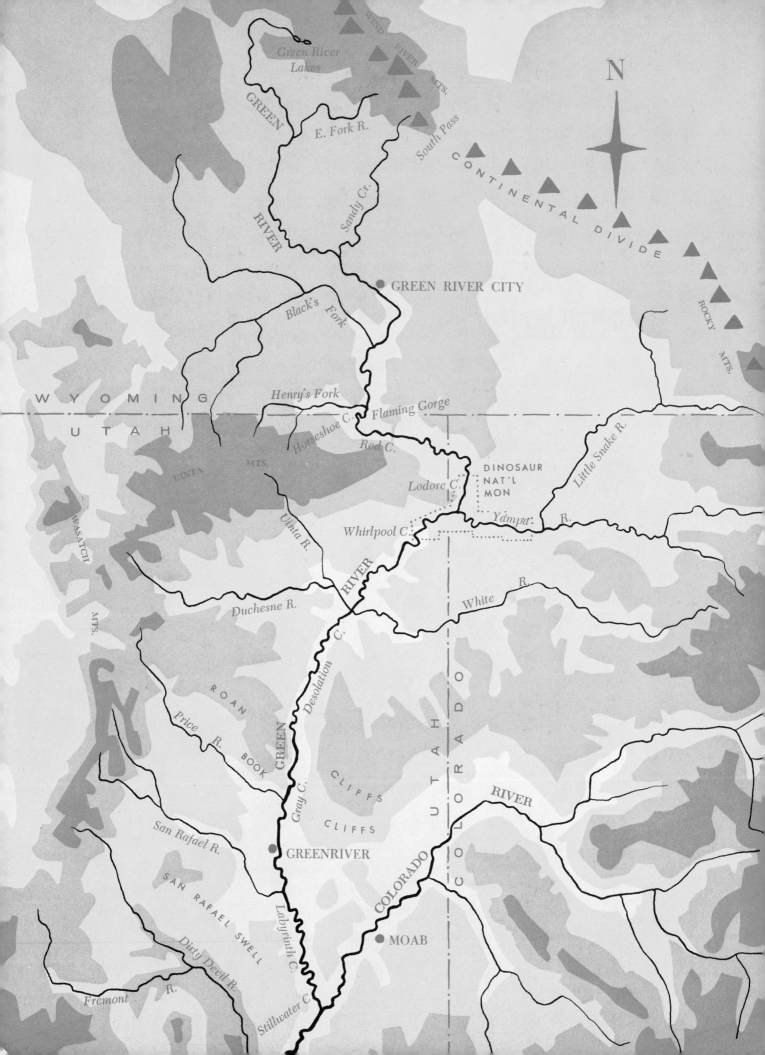

All things have a beginning.

A river must begin where vapor has condensed over a sloping surface to produce a running-off of water. In great ranges of mountains, whose peaks reach high into the storms, this condition prevails. During cold seasons the moisture is stored as snowpack until warm air unlocks the crystals. Then, as the snow melts, tiny rivulets grow by stages into roaring cataracts, and these carry fragments of rock downward in their torrent. Thus, in infancy the river acquires an abrasive weapon with which it can move mountains—a grain of sand. If the slope is steep enough, it will have the power to convert pebbles into grindstones. If it grinds steadily enough, it will be able to cut through the hardest rock for thousands of feet, and continue to cut like a knife in a spreading wound, until it has reduced the mountains, valleys, plateaus and bottomlands of its entire drainage to mean sea level. This is the significance and the fate of such a river as the Colorado and its tributaries, unless counteracted by great changes in the earth itself.

SOURCE OF THE GREEN RIVER

The life history of the Green River follows the dynamic pattern of all Western Slope rivers. This parent of the Colorado has its origin among the Wind River Mountains of Wyoming, which

A Mountain
Stream
Comes of Age

3

came into existence as a great earth fold about seventy million years ago. Involved in the folding were layers of sedimentary rocks deposited on the floor of ancient seas over a period of several hundred million years. This accumulation of marine sediment was exposed to erosive forces as a result of the folding, and in time the arched layers were worn away to expose the granite core of the range. At a still later time the mass was again uplifted and re-exposed by glaciers and powerful streams. During the glacial period, twin basins were scooped from the granite to form natural reservoirs for the small scattered sources of the Green River. Near these gem-like lakes wild life abounds, particularly within the protected Bridger Wilderness Area which embraces the high valleys and mountain summits. This region is a division of Bridger National Forest, which includes the western slope of the Wind River range and parent watershed of the Green River. It has been a national preserve since 1891, when President Harrison set aside a huge tract of public land for the first timber and watershed conservation project—the Yellowstone Timberland Reserve, of which the Bridger Forest was part.

GREEN RIVER BASIN OF WYOMING: EXPLORATION BY LAND

The Wind River mountains and their foothills had been a favorite Indian hunting ground for centuries before the coming of white trappers in the 1820's. During the brief advent of the fur trade these unique frontiersmen overran the Green and all of its tributaries north of the Uinta Basin; this period of the river's history is a chronicle of the fur people and their institutions. Meanwhile, the westward migration of settlers was gathering force, and the mounting demand for an established route of travel —well mapped and described—became a serious concern of the United States government. As a result, several geographic surveys

4

of the country west of the Great Plains were organized by the War and Interior Departments. Among these was the initial expedition of "The Pathfinder," John C. Fremont, then twenty-nine and a lieutenant in the Topographic Corps of the War Department. In 1842 this colorful geographer and his party, under the guidance of famed Rocky Mountain scout Kit Carson, crossed the Continental Divide at South Pass on the Oregon Trail, turned northward into the upper Green River basin, and proceeded to make a general exploration of the Wind River range. There is no mention of the Green River in Fremont's report of this expedition. He did, however note the shining network of streams and ponds which line the western Wind River slopes and which flow ultimately into the Green. He wrote, "It seemed as if, from the vast expanse of uninteresting prairie we had passed over, Nature had collected all the beauties together in one chosen place. We were overlooking a deep valley which was entirely occupied by three lakes, and from the brink the surrounding ridges rose precipitously five hundred and a thousand feet, covered with the dark green of the balsam pine, relieved on the border of the lakes with the light foliage of the aspen . . . the green of the waters, common to lakes of great depth, showed that it would be impossible to cross them." The Green River was mentioned by its Spanish name, "Rio Verde," in Fremont's account of his 1843-44 explorations; but then, as now, the derivation was unknown.

PIONEER CROSSROADS

From its origin in Wind River country the Green flows southward on a gentle gradient through a broad arid basin which occupies the greater part of southwestern Wyoming. The soft sedimentary rocks which cover most of the region have given the landscape its typical "badlands" topography—low ragged cliffs

A Mountain
Stream
Comes of Age

5

and hills in subdued colors—and have yielded rich deposits of animal and plant fossils, as well as oil, gas, and minerals of high commercial value. In our time this semi-wasteland is crossed by railroad and continental highway, and supports a large grazing industry as well as several population centers. During the early 1800's it afforded an easy passage between mountain ranges to westward-bound pioneers, explorers, and traders. In consequence, the routes of the California Trail, the Oregon Trail of 1843, the Mormon Trail of 1847, the Overland Stage Route, the Original Pony Express, the Overland Trail, and the route of Captain Bonneville may be traced through the upper Green River basin. Most of these trails led north and west from Independence, Missouri, ascending the Missouri and Platte Rivers, then tracing the Sweetwater River from its mouth in central Wyoming to headwaters just below the Continental Divide. They crossed the Divide by way of South Pass, at the southern extremity of the Wind River range. Upon reaching Green River valley below the pass, the trails separated and continued south and west toward their several destinations, crossing the Green at a number of points which are still identified as ford and ferry sites.

THE "OLD ONES"

It is usual to think of important archaeological findings in the Colorado River Basin as being largely confined to that part of the basin which lies below the Green-Colorado River confluence. However, other prehistoric cultures existed in the country north of this zone, extending as far as the upper Green River watershed in Wyoming. Dwellings, manufactured articles of many kinds, and a profusion of petroglyphs dated prior to 1100 A.D. have been discovered throughout this area. The most important of these cultures, the Fremont, differs from the higher Pueblo culture of

6

the Southwest, though some contact existed between these. The Green River basin has yielded still another extremely valuable site which represents a primitive culture (Yuma) of perhaps 10,000 years ago. North of Rock Springs, Wyoming, and in Black's Fork valley were found knife blades and tools in a deposit thought to be postglacial. This means that the Green River and its environs have been of importance to humans for a very long time.

The Fur Trade and Explorations By River Boat

Near the present town of Daniel, Wyoming, the river meanders through a wide valley bounded by low hills. The luxuriant growth of trees and grass in this basin-within-a-basin vividly contrasts the brown desert country which stretches away from its edges as far as the eye can see. These inviting meadows were the scene of a unique wilderness institution—the "General Rendezvous" of the fur industry—during which thousands of red and white trappers poured in from their solitary haunts to meet, with traders from the East, for a grand orgy of trading and all manner of wild carousal. Six of these extravaganzas took place here between 1825 and 1840, under the aegis of General William H. Ashley. The General, a former army officer and politician in the States, interested himself in the fur business early in the 1820's. His advertisement in a St. Louis newspaper soliciting "one hundred young men to ascend the Missouri River to its source, there to be employed for one, two or three years", opened the organized phase of beaver trapping in the Green River Basin. Among Ashley's first hundred were Jim Bridger, the "Daniel Boone of the Rockies", William Sublette, Jedediah Smith, Etienne Provot, and others whose names became legend in the annals of scouting and mountaineering in the West. On the General's return from his second recruiting trip in the States in 1825, the loss of his horses led him to divide the party and set out with a small group traveling down the Green River in "bullboats", constructed on the spot by stretching buffalo hides over a willow framework. On his way down the river he designated the mouth of Henry's Fork near Flaming Gorge as a location for the first "general rendezvous" of his company, and continuing downstream through the upper canyons of the Green River, survived rapids, starvation, and other severe hardships associated with inexperience and primitive equipment. Then, instead of ending the voyage at an established trappers' camp in Brown's Hole, as expected, Ashley had grown so fascinated with river exploration that he plunged and portaged on down through Lodore, Whirlpool, and Split Mountain Canyons. He continued his search for beaver into the Uintah Basin to a point about fifty miles below the mouth of the Duchesne River (then called the Uintah), where he finally left his frail, battered boats and obtained horses from some Indians for his return to the place of rendezvous via the Uinta Mountains, thus completing the first venture of white man into the mysterious Uinta canyons which lie south of the Wyoming basin.

A score of years later, young Billy Manly and six cohorts, impatient with the pace of their California-bound prairie schooner, recommissioned an old ferryboat which they found at one of the Green River trail crossings, and set off down the Green—confident of making better time to the Pacific coast by this route. Their boat did not survive Red Canyon, but they hewed some primitive craft from large pines near the wreck and went thumping and churning on down the river through Lodore, Split Mountain, Desolation and Gray Canyons. However, they elected to give up the voyage near present Greenriver, Utah, after they were tendered a graphic prediction of the approaching dangers by a Ute chieftain.

Torrent in the Desert

Following another lapse of twenty years, Major John Wesley Powell launched his history-making first Colorado River expedition in 1869 at the recently completed rail crossing in Green River City, Wyoming. With four special cataract boats, by modern standards badly designed and overloaded, Powell and his party of nine undertook exploration of the canyons of the Green and Colorado Rivers as far as the mouth of the Virgin River in northwestern Arizona. In addition to his experience as a school teacher and army officer, Powell was a professional geologist and geographer, and had traveled the full length of the Mississippi, Ohio, and Illinois Rivers by boat. He had just completed two years of geographic study in the mountains east and north of the Upper Colorado basin. Thus, although he lacked experience in white-water navigation, he was uniquely qualified to lead this daring survey. From his collection of data regarding the river canyons and adjacent country he surely had a clear conception of the dangerous nature of the Colorado; yet he approached the task with assurance, enthusiasm, and unquenchable curiosity. Most of his boatmen met the successive challenges of perilous rapids, severe weather, back-breaking labor complicated by chronic starvation, and personal insecurity with a fortitude that seemed beyond human limitations.

It might be supposed that, once having accomplished this unparalleled feat, the one-armed Powell would have pursued his scientific career in more sedentary fields. However, his first voyage was shortened from ten to three months because of the wrecking of a boat and loss of food and supplies; also, sample collections had to be left behind and valuable records were lost. For this reason Powell sought and obtained support for a second expedition to complete the scientific work left undone. This second survey,

A Mountain Stream Comes of Age

made in 1871-72, covered in extensive detail the same segments of the river as the first, except the portion between Kanab Creek and the Virgin, and include wide land excursions to the north of the Colorado from the Dirty Devil watershed to Virgin River country below the Grand Canyon. The surveyors also visited the seven Hopi mesa towns east of Grand Canyon; Walter C. Powell, a cousin of the Major, has left us a priceless account of this tour. The journals kept by Major Powell and members of both expeditions provide not only the first coherent description of the Colorado River and its environs, but also an appraisal of men and their relationships in an elemental situation.

Henry's Fork

Torrent in the Desert

Southward from Green River City the river follows a placid, winding course among greatly eroded treeless hills punctuated by isolated needle-like buttes and cliff remnants a few hundred feet high. From the west two large mountain streams which rise on the northern Uinta slopes make their contribution to the young river—Black's and Henry's Forks. The latter, discribed by Stephen Jones of the second Powell expedition as "the most crooked stream I ever saw," winds its last few miles through a broad sunbaked plain and empties into the river at the upstream margin of Flaming Gorge. This spot was used as a campsite by trappers and wayfarers for many years and was selected by General Ashley as a meeting place for his fur trappers in the 1820's, when the Green River Basin was still a haunt of the beaver.

Flaming Gorge, Portal of the Uinta Canyons

Mounting abruptly from the flat land surrounding Henry's Fork, a craggy scooped-out ridge flanks the river's north bank at

10

the head of a long S-curve. An apt description of the Gorge was provided by one of Powell's men—"a pass through the rocks which are of red sandstone and look very much like a flame in the rays of the sun." It is in reality the gateway to a long series of canyons traversing the eastern end of the Uinta mountains. In distinction to other streams of the Uinta region, the Green River follows a course strikingly out of accord with local topography as it passes through, rather than around, the steeply inclined strata of the range. This anomaly may be explained by assuming that the river established its course in younger, relatively soft sedimentary layers which overlaid the resistant rock of the present canyons. Gradually the soft rocks were worn away and, with uplift of the region, the Green entrenched its course in the underlying hard layers. There is evidence to suggest that the present channel of the Green River was not a continuous watercourse until some time after the rising of the Uinta mountains and subsequent collapse of the eastern end of this great arch. Stream flow across the Uinta axis was obstructed by the rising land, perhaps to the extent of lake formation. Collapse of the uplift in the Brown's Park-Lodore region greatly influenced the behavior of local streams, so that a more active watershed might "capture" an adjoining one and change the course of its flow. It is postulated that developments of this nature may have led the ancestral Green River to its seemingly impossible penetration of the Uinta highlands, although so much geologic evidence has been effaced by erosion that this fascinating story may never be fully known.

Viewed from upstream, the jagged cliffs of Flaming Gorge present a startling change in the landscape, which was variously commented upon by the early river travelers. William Manly and his frightened party believed that the water disappeared through some mysterious outlet under the wall of mountains ahead. The

A Mountain Stream Comes of Age

journalist later wrote in his memoirs that he had resigned himself in that moment to resuming the westward trek afoot, "for I did not propose to follow the river down any sort of hole into any mountain." The boatmen soon found, however, that the Green merely turned a corner, and proceeded downstream to meet the real challenge of many rapids before they finally conceded mastery to the river.

HORSESHOE CANYON

After its gyration through Flaming Gorge, the Green rounds a long curve where highly colored cliffs stand back a quarter mile from the banks, then abruptly enters Horseshoe Canyon. Here the rushing water has cut through 2500 feet of cream-colored coal-bearing rock, leaving nearly perpendicular walls on both sides. Many unbroken stone faces a thousand feet or more in height soar skyward from the tawny current. In two and a half miles the channel completes a half-circle bend. This gorge was called "Canyon of the Rapid" by the first Powell expedition, since it contained the first rapid they encountered—a roaring one with a drop of several feet. However, the canyon was referred to as the "Horseshoe" by members of the second expedition, and this name has persisted.

RED CANYON

From the lower end of Horseshoe Canyon the banks recede to form an irregular channel for about six miles, into which several mountain streams empty their crystal cargo. The Green crosses the axis of the Uinta fault at this point, which is plainly evident in the sharp inclination of the bent rock layers in surrounding cliffs. The walls then close in as the river breaches another uplift to form Red Canyon—a thirty-mile chasm of rose-colored sand-

Torrent in the Desert

12

stone whose steep broken bluffs rise directly from the water except where small wooded "parks" intervene. Here graceful pines, junipers, and cottonwoods ornament the gorge, and the water is turbulent throughout much of the canyon's length. Ashley's Falls, one of the greater rapids in Red Canyon, was so named because General Ashley painted his inscription on a boulder nearby as he passed in 1825. This message was still legible when Major Powell visited Red Canyon almost half a century later. Near Ashley's Falls the aforementioned Manly party lost its ferryboat and had to continue by dugout. The tumultuous waters are soon to be impounded by a 490-foot multi-purpose Bureau of Reclamation dam. The reservoir will extend 91 miles upstream through part of Red Canyon itself, Horseshoe Canyon and Flaming Gorge; raising the water level to the doorstep of Green River City, Wyoming. Unlike other dams of the Colorado watershed, this one and its reservoir lie within a national forest—the Ashley. An elaborate system of campgrounds, boat docks, and other facilities for public recreational use has been developed by the U.S. Forest Service.

BROWN'S PARK

Emerging from Red Canyon, the river curves southeastward through Brown's Hole, a rolling hill-girt valley about thirty miles in length and ten miles wide, whose floor is invaded by an arm of the adjacent mountains, so that the Green River forms a brief canyon within it. This was named Swallow Canyon by Major Powell because of the many birds which nested in its cliffs. The spacious meadows of Brown's Hole had served as a campsite and gathering place for Indians, trappers, and wayfarers many years before it was visited and described by Powell in 1869. Fort Davy Crockett, one of the principal Western Slope fur trading posts, was founded

A Mountain
Stream
Comes of Age

13

at the Hole about 1837 by a group of independent trappers. The Fort passed through the hands of various owners and ultimately declined with depletion of beaver colonies in the Green River basin. During its heyday Fort Davy Crockett was a mecca for travelers as well as men in the fur trade, located as it was on one of the transcontinental routes. At the time Powell visited the Hole it was used chiefly as a grazing area for large herds of cattle on their way from Texas to California, and in the '90's it became a notorious hideaway for outlaws. One of the large flat-topped mountains which adjoin Brown's Hole to the south marks the site of a fantastic hoax perpetrated by a pair of prospectors who "seeded" a large tract with uncut inferior gems, as the basis of a huge land-leasing operation. This locale is still known as Diamond Mountain, though with the passing years Brown's Hole has assumed the more conventional name of Brown's Park.

LODORE CANYON

From this valley which has seen so much of the human drama the Green abruptly enters the easternmost flank of the Uintas, a system of high plateaus broken by isolated ridges and peaks. The Lodore, as this canyon was poetically baptized by Major Powell, is a dark narrow opening through the mountains, whose "gates" rise sharply from the rolling meadows of Brown's Park to a towering height of 2100 feet. The reddish-brown sandstone blocks which form its steep walls are decked with sage and juniper, augmented by patches of pine and spruce, but there is scant forest to abate the starkness of Lodore. The turbulent water, whose usual color is that of buckskin, drops four hundred feet in this sixteen-mile canyon to form one of the steepest extended gradients in the Green River. The first Powell party required ten days to navigate the gorge, including several days the men spent in camp resting,

14

drying out, and putting things in order. George Bradley wrote, between portages, "The scenery at this point is sublime. The red sandstone rises on either side more than 2000 feet, shutting out the sun for much of the day, while at our feet the river, lashed to foam, rushes on with indescribable fury." He also had a word to say about one of the less comodious campsites: "If I had a dog that would lie where my bed is tonight I would kill him and burn his collar and swear I never owned him." It is not surprising to find here rapids dubbed "Disaster Falls," where Powell lost a boat and its contents, and "Hell's Half Mile," where the gorge is so choked with great boulders that even today's skilled rivermen with modern equipment find severe hazards. This rapid, along with Lava Falls of Grand Canyon, is often portaged.

ECHO PARK

The river emerges from the red pit of Lodore to enter the confines of Echo Park. This crescent-shaped valley is the site of an ancient geologic fault where the earth's crust fractured and slipped, leaving the cream-colored Weber sandstone exposed at river level within the Park, whereas in the upthrust portion the same layer tops an eroded plateau 2500 feet above. Steamboat Rock, so called for its profile, is a mile-long monolith which juts into an amphitheater formed by vertical cliffs enclosing several hundred acres of grassy bottomland; the walls are breached only by a single wash, the entering and emerging Green River, and the mouth of the Yampa River, which joins the Green here. This shut-in valley is part of a large tract lying in bottoms of the Yampa and Green Rivers, known as Pat's Hole. The "Hole" was the chosen habitat of hermit Pat Lynch, who occupied various caves and shelters for several decades and left his indelible imprint here. The descriptive name of Echo Park was suggested to the

A Mountain
Stream
Comes of Age

15

Powell boatmen by multiple echoes at Steamboat Rock. More recently this name has designated a controversial damsite on the Green, which may yet pass the legislative barrier.

THE YAMPA

Directly opposite Steamboat Rock to the east, the Yampa or Bear River, largest tributary of the Green, unites with the latter after a long, tortuous journey from the Rabbit-Ears country of mountainous northwestern Colorado state. The lower reaches of this beautiful small river were first explored by white men in 1871, when five members of the second Powell expedition rowed and towed their boats twelve miles upstream, marvelling at the geologic and topographic features of Bear Canyon, with its close-set vertical walls of towering ivory sandstone and its exquisitely forested bottomlands or "parks." This handsome canyon is now a favored location for river-boating enthusiasts in times of high water.

WHIRLPOOL CANYON AND ISLAND PARK

After a sharp U-turn around Steamboat Rock, the Green River bends at once to the west and enters Whirlpool Canyon, where the tawny water, increased in volume and power by the Yampa, is sent rushing into eddies by rocky buttresses and small bends. The river bed drops only 100 feet in eight and a half miles, but the broken channel makes for rough passage. Jagged limestone peaks top the craggy 2000-foot red sandstone walls, adding a nightmarish quality to the scene. The river emerges from Whirlpool into a valley of green bottomlands enclosed on the north by low, barren hills or "badlands", and on the south by an arm of the Yampa Plateau. Here the Green seems to lose itself among numerous islands formed by the cutting of new channels

16

during high water. This basin, appropriately named "Island Park," is the site of a geologic fold, where great compressive forces caused the horizontal earth layers to bend and break; remnants of the broken strata are found standing almost on end. Giant cottonwoods ornament the level rangeland of the valley floor. General Ashley recorded the presence of buffalo in Island Park during his 1825 voyage, and other large pastoral species have been observed there from time to time. Powell's first survey party picked currants and shot "a fine large buck as fat as beef" in Island Park to augment their dwindling provisions. A foot trail leads from the Park over the badlands to a remote and lovely corner of the Dinosaur Monument, known as Jones Hole. This deep cleft in the creamy sandstone is transformed into a lush fisherman's paradise by Jones Hole Creek, a fair-sized mountain stream which joins the Green River two and a half miles below. This "hole", like many another small isolated canyon in the eastern Uinta country, has served as a hideout for fugitives.

Split Mountain

Following on the heels of Island Park is perhaps the most provocative of the many striking topographic forms seen in the Green River watershed—Split Mountain. The mountain appears to have been a contiguous land mass before the uplift which accelerated the river's downcutting activity. Thus, the stream enters from the north, turns west immediately to carve its way through five miles of the mountain's core, then emerges onto a low plain by turning 90 degrees southward; a Z-shaped gorge 2600 feet deep is formed by this unusual meander. The north half of the mountain also has a dry cleft some 1400 feet deep paralleling the river's entrance, which suggests a geomorphic change antedating the Green River. Another feature of interest is found at the lower

A Mountain
Stream
Comes of Age

17

end of the gorge, where the exposed massive sandstone is fantastically eroded into great towers and curved shelves. This amazing formation may be seen for many miles along Ashley Valley to the south, where a major highway crosses the Green River near Jensen, Utah. Split Mountain has been designated as a possible damsite, and future generations may visit this canyon to view a man-made spectacle.

DINOSAUR NATIONAL MONUMENT

Among the folded strata at Split Mountain Canyon's mouth many fossil bones and partial skeletons of dinosaurs have been excavated from the Morrison formation (age about 130 million years). The Dinosaur Monument, established in 1915, originally consisted of eighty acres containing the fossil deposit. It was expanded in 1938 to include the spectacular canyon country surrounding Green River from the head of Lodore Canyon through Split Mountain Gorge, as well as a large tract extending eastward up the Yampa. It is planned that the splendid canyons of the Monument will become more accessible through development of Park Service roads and facilities.

ESCALANTE'S CROSSING OF THE GREEN

Near the Dinosaur quarry is the site of an old river crossing and campground much used by Indians, traders, and other travelers of the "early days." In 1871 the Powell party camped at this place, a few miles below the grove of cottonwoods whose ancestors had sheltered Father Escalante almost a century earlier, during his celebrated exploratory mission in the wilderness of Utah, Colorado, and Arizona. The Padre and his companions made their only intentional crossing of the Green at this point on September 14, 1776. He wrote in his journal of the "six black cottonwoods"

18

under which the party camped, barely mentioning the ford, which must have been at extremely low water level.

DESOLATION CANYON

The Uintah Basin is trenched from north to south by the Green River. Beginning at the base of the Uinta Mountains and their neighboring plateaus to the east, this region is an arid land of low, barren hills, "badland" cliffs, and scant vegetation. For many centuries before the coming of white men, the Basin's only inhabitants were semi-sedentary Indian tribes who made their dwellings, hunted animals, and sometimes raised small crops on land adjoining the watercourses. Even today the region's sparse settlement is found along the Green River and its few perennial tributaries, which derive most of their water from distant sources among the Wasatch, Uinta, and western Rocky Mountains. The Basin's southward-rising rim, known as the Tavaputs Plateau, is cleft into eastern and western halves by the Green River. For ninety miles the river cuts down through the slopes of this plateau to form Desolation Canyon. Distinguished by scarcity of plant life and by the angular lines of its cliffs and buttes, this linked series of "badland" canyons was named "Desolation" by Almon Thompson of the second Powell expedition. The only verdure seen is near the waterline and consists chiefly of sage, juniper, and greasewood with rare cottonwoods and clumps of willow or tamarack. The land recedes from the river in great terraces, intricately broken by lateral canyons and gulches. The rocks, which appear drab-colored at a distance, prove to be of many hues. In numerous places the canyon walls have eroded into fantastic forms which resemble castles, cathedrals, and minarets. Though Desolation is less frequented by river expeditions than other canyons of the Green and the Colorado, it contains a high

A Mountain
Stream
Comes of Age

19

percentage of turbulent water and a number of formidable rapids, particularly during high-water season.

Gray Canyon: Price River

Near the end of Desolation Canyon, where its cliffs reach their maximum height, a striking change is seen. The lofty plateau breaks to form its first terrace, the Roan Cliffs, which strike at right angles to the river; the valley widens and verdure appears in the bottoms. The red sandstone of the canyon walls is replaced by fossil-bearing shale and conglomerate rocks. Numerous deposits of coal appear among thin-bedded sandstone in the low bluffs, suggesting the names of "Coal Canyon" and "Gray Canyon" which have been applied to this gorge. Fourteen miles above its abrupt ending in the Book Cliffs, the lower terrace of the Tavaputs Plateau, Gray Canyon is breached from the west by Price River. The Price, a typical plateau stream, rises along the eastern slopes of the Wasatch Plateau and curiously amputates the extreme southwestern tip of the West Tavaputs table here. At the mouth of Gray Canyon a wooden waterwheel lifts Green River water from a shallow impoundment into a local irrigation system for dry range at the foot of the Book Cliffs.

Gunnison's Crossing

In the broad filled-in valley lying just south of the Book Cliffs, the Green River flows through another community which bears its name—Greenriver, Utah. This town is located near the river crossing of the old Spanish Trail from Santa Fe to Los Angeles, used by many of the nineteenth-century pathfinders. In 1853 ill-fated Captain John Gunnison followed this trail across the Green during his exploration of a southern route for the proposed Pacific Railroad; the crossing was known as Gunnison's

Crossing for many years thereafter. General Fremont's fifth expedition, designed to test the practicability of a 38th-parallel roadway route during winter, used this ford in 1854. In the following year Mormon colonists bound for the Moab mission also made their crossing of the Green at this point. The river is now bridged by a railroad and a continental highway at the historic trail site.

Labyrinth Canyon; San Rafael River

From Gunnison's Crossing the river winds southward along the eastern margin of the San Rafael area, cutting deeper and deeper into the tiled rock layers which form the walls of another major canyon—the Labyrinth. To the west of this canyon lies the Green River Desert, to the east a high peninsular plateau which ends at the junction of the Green and Upper Colorado Rivers. The small, alkaline San Rafael River threads its way eastward from the foot of the Wasatch Plateau, through that wierdly dissected dome-shaped earth fold, the San Rafael Swell, to join the Green near the head of Labyrinth Canyon. In this twisting gorge a mild current flows between stately burnt-orange sandstone bluffs and buttes which rise vertically above steep slopes of buff-colored talus. At some points the canyon walls are close-set, elsewhere they range far distant from the water's edge, leaving room for wide bottomlands. The river's meandering course is strikingly typified at "Bowknot Bend," where the channel forms a gooseneck so narrow that a single butte stands isolated within the almost completed circle of moving water. Labyrinth's pattern of descent testifies that the Green was a wandering pastoral stream in this region before uplift of the land caused cutting of the canyon. The richness of the soil washed down from the upper watershed and deposited here is manifest in lush green plants which grow in every place touched by moisture from the river. In addi-

A Mountain
Stream
Comes of Age

21

tion to its unusual scenic values, Labyrinth Canyon has been found to contain uranium, which was extensively mined in some sections of the canyon itself; oil and gas have been recovered from plateau lands nearby.

UPHEAVAL DOME

An unusual and little-known feature of the Junction Plateau, on its west rim near the division between Labyrinth and Stillwater Canyons, is a crater-like geologic structure having a maximum depth of four hundred feet—Upheaval Dome. This interesting phenomenon, two miles in diameter, consists of an eroded dome encircled by a trough or "sink", whose color is an elaborate confusion of blue, green, red, chocolate, and saffron; this is wholly enclosed by a high red sandstone ridge except for a drainage way which empties directly into the Green River. The concentric colored zones of the dome represent the several rock formations involved in the upheaval. Though this resembles a "crypto-volcanic" structure, it is now thought to have been formed by the upward pressure and associated displacements of a large salt plug near the surface of the earth, rather than by explosion of volcanic gases. No evidence of volcanic rock has been found to support an explosive origin of the structure. It is expected that Upheaval Dome, together with Grand View and Dead Horse Points, which are other landmarks of the Junction plateau, will become a Utah state recreation area.

STILLWATER CANYON

A short distance below the Upheaval drainage canyon the river runs down through the lower part of the orange sandstone, then through several other variously-colored formations whose shelves break away from the channel in widening tiers, and finally penetrates a thick layer of buff-colored stone which identifies the terminal Stillwater Canyon. Here the walls come closer to the river and more nearly vertical than in the Labyrinth. This remote canyon, like many another in the Colorado basin, was inhabited by aboriginal peoples. Members of the first Powell expedition found Indian ruins in crevices of the canyon walls and surmised, improbably, that the occupants had departed less than fifty years before. Contrary to Powell's belief that his was the first party of white men to navigate the rivers in the Junction area, several cliff inscriptions of Denis Julien, discovered in later years, attest that this daring mountaineer and trapper passed through Stillwater and Cataract Canyons by boat in 1836. From 1891 to 1897 these canyons were cruised infrequently by a 35-foot steam yacht, the "Major Powell," first power boat used on the Green River. The usual itinerary was a round trip from the San Rafael's mouth to the first rapid in Cataract, but other reports indicate she went to Moab and even, incredibly, to the foot of Cataract Canyon.

The Junction

Subsequent to the visits of Julien and Powell, only a few river adventurers and surveyors observed the actual junction of the Green and Colorado Rivers before the recent advent of the neoprene raft and motorboat, as well as construction of uranium access roads on the lower shelves of the Junction plateau. Both of Powell's groups camped at the confluence and scaled the adjacent cliffs to record scientific data regarding this important feature of the Colorado basin. In the words of Almon Thompson, "The junction . . . is in a canyon with walls on all sides 800 feet, nearly vertical . . . I think a prettier joining of two streams to form a third was never seen. Neither absorbs or flows into the other

A Mountain
Stream
Comes of Age

23

but like two forces of equal strength they mingle and unite." Above the inner canyon rise the many-terraced walls of colored stone, exposed for more than 2000 feet from water level to the top of the adjoining plateau. Far back from the convergent channels of the Green and Upper Colorado Rivers, the elaborate design of the land is crowned by the tall, stately orange cliffs. Their crumbled fragments combine with those of lesser formations to form long talus slopes reaching down to the "White Rim," a broad scalloped shelf whose sandstone has withstood the nibbling of erosion longer than softer layers above and beneath. Intricate canyon systems lace the landscape, with solitary mesas and great buttes standing like monuments to the ancient seas in which they were formed. Red mingles with pink and orange; distant glimpses of the sky-reflecting rivers are set in emerald garlands of the inner canyon, while elsewhere the occasional juniper and sage alone relieve the desert's severity. An ever-present veil of blue tints the distant profile and swathes the horizon. Especially as low rays from the sun intensify colors and lengthen shadows, this desert citadel of the mighty river seems to belong to another world, another millennium.

Torrent in the Desert

24

Green River Lakes

Upper Green River Basin

*Slide Lake, near the
Green River's Source*

*Beaver Pond in the Wind
River Mountains*

Near Site of Old Mormon Ferry Crossing

Old Lombard Ferry Site

At Green River City, Wyoming

*Henry's Fork joins the
Green River*

*Flaming Gorge, seen from
the Boar's Tusk*

Approach to Flaming Gorge

Horseshoe Canyon

*Red Canyon and the
Uinta Highland*

Brown's Park

Vermillion Creek

The Gates of Lodore

Lodore Canyon

Echo Park

Bear Canyon

The Upper Yampa in Spring Flood

*Yampa River near
Echo Park
(facing page)*

Green River cuts through
Split Mountain

Whirlpool Canyon
(facing page)

Island Park

*Father Escalante's Crossing
Near Split Mountain*

*Desolation Canyon
(facing page)*

Rapid in Gray Canyon

Price River
(facing page)

*Weir at the Foot of
Gray Canyon*

*Waterwheel near
Greenriver, Utah*

Labyrinth Canyon

San Rafael River

Boating in Labyrith Canyon

Upheaval Dome

Marathon Racer in Stillwater Canyon

*The White Rim from
Grand View Point*

*Stormy Vista from
Junction Plateau
(facing page)*

*Confluence of the Green and
Upper Colorado Rivers*

Chapter 2

From the Rooftops
of the Continent

"Colorado" is one of several

descriptive and commemorative names given the river by Spanish explorers of the sixteenth and seventeenth centuries. Only one other early name was related to the river itself—"Rio del Tizon" or River of the Firebrand. Diaz, a Coronado captain, used this term because he encountered some Indians along the banks who carried torches, for warmth or possibly to repel insects. The other European names had meaning only within the personal reference of those who applied them, and thus did not achieve general usage—River of Good Faith; River of the Martyrs; River of Good Guidance.

The Colorado was commonly referred to in the descriptive sense as "the red river" among Europeans who had seen it during times of heavy runoff, when much of the red-tinged soil of its watershed was swept along in the tide. Father Francisco Garces, however, was the first to crystallize the term "colorado" into a proper name by consistent use of it in his writing. This eighteenth-century Franciscan also made the significant observation that from the land of the Utes (eastern part of the Great Basin) to the river's final outpouring into the Gulf of California "it gathers to itself no notable body of water; wherefore it is likely that the greater part of its abundance comes from far beyond." As we know, the principal sources of the Colorado are located in the high mountainous

From the Roof= tops of the Continent

59

backbone of the continent—far north and east of Garces' territory —where the Grand, the Green, and their chief tributaries rise.

Thus, the name which survived is a direct reference to one of the river's native qualities—that burden of red-brown soil particles which, as cause and effect, distinguishes the Colorado from other great rivers of the world.

Origin of the Colorado

Like the Green River, the Upper Colorado springs from snowbanks of the Continental Divide. Its headwaters drain a great crescent-shaped basin on the Pacific slope of the Divide in north central Colorado state. The broad arch or fold which later became the Rocky Mountains was pushed up by disruptive forces within the earth's crust about seventy-five million years ago, coincident with the last recession of the seas. This uplifting was accompanied for a time by outpourings of lava and volcanic eruptions, which blanketed much of the Rocky Mountain region. Periods of erosion alternated with upward movements of the mountainous areas. The sculpturing process was further influenced by climatic fluctuations; at various times the mountains were gouged and scoured by glaciers, and alluvial deposits accumulated in basins between the mountain ranges when the inland climate became more arid. The Colorado River system, although fairly well established, in some geologists' opinion, by the mid-Miocene period (about twelve million years ago), was interrupted by regional tilting of the land surface; only since the late Pliocene (about eight million years ago) have the river channels been reoccupied and cut deeper into the earth. The Colorado has a long history of headward erosion, capture of other drainage areas, and the breaching of upstream basins to form the integrated system of today. The Rocky Mountain region has continued to rise intermittently to the present time, giving impetus to the valley- and canyon-making activity of streams in the Colorado River drainage, and has evolved into the intricate highland pattern which surrounds the river today.

WATER-USE SYSTEMS AND THE NATIONAL PARK

The mountain peaks of the Colorado Rockies, now 12,000 to 14,000 feet above sea level, capture great volumes of moisture drawn inland from the Gulf of Mexico by barometric "lows" which constantly swirl over them. Numerous streams carry the runoff into narrow Kawuneeche Valley, where the Colorado's "north fork" takes the form of many marshes and ponds linked by a small, obscure channel. As the valley widens and the mountain barrier on the west diminishes into foothills, the river enters a system of reservoirs including Granby, Shadow Mountain, and Grand Lakes, which provide the source of irrigation water and electric power to the upper South Platte River Basin east of the Rockies, as part of the Colorado-Big Thompson Project. Water is pumped from Willow Creek, a small downstream tributary, up to the level of Granby Reservoir, then one more step to Shadow Mountain and Grand Lakes, where it enters the 13-mile Alva B. Adams tunnel. By this conduit a portion of the Colorado's water naturally destined for the Pacific is carried through the granite heart of the Rockies to the Atlantic drainage, where it brings verdant growth to three-quarters of a million acres of dry farmland, and electric power to communities in east central Colorado state. This withdrawn water is replaced to the Colorado River by the regulated discharge from two downstream dams located on tributary streams, the Green Mountain and Williams Fork Dams. Other transmountain diversions of Colorado River water pass eastward to Denver and north into the Poudre Valley.

Grand Lake, sometimes called the source of the Colorado

61

River, is a large moraine lake which drains a broad glacier-ravaged area among the high summits of the Divide. Together with its associated reservoirs, it forms one of the most picturesque recreation areas of the continent. Nestled at the foot of the snow-crowned Rockies, this lake affords the highest yacht anchorage in the world and is part of the western limit of Rocky Mountain National Park.

The park, comprising 410 square miles of the highest mountain terrain in this region, provides an open record of the raw materials and forces which formed the great continental watersheds. The carved summits and rolling uplands above 12,000 feet, the broad U-shaped valleys, the altitude and distribution of various rock layers tell the story of ancient times. Today's flowering alpine meadows, virgin forests, streams and lakes—and the life that is in them—write another chapter of the earth's biography. A large part of this magnificent wilderness has been made accessible to the public through fifty years of planned development. Numerous roads and trails reach into the canyons and cross the highlands. Now even the passing motorist can gaze down upon a hundred million years of recent history and, threading through it like a silvery hair, one of its most powerful agents—the Colorado River.

EARLY HISTORY OF COLORADO HEADWATERS

The massive core of the Rocky Mountains which occupies the central portion of Colorado state gives rise to four great river systems—the two forks of the Platte and the Arkansas to the east, the Rio Grande to the south, the San Juan to the southwest, and westward the Colorado. This rocky wilderness proved more attractive and approachable to white men by way of the Arkansas River or from the Spanish towns of New Mexico than over the uncharted expanse of plateau land to the west, with its hostile

62

Utes and lack of water. Thus it was that the headwaters of the Arkansas, Platte, and Rio Grande were overrun with trappers and adventurers by the 1820's, while those of the Colorado remained almost unknown.

The earliest recorded expedition to this remote region was that of James Ohio Pattie, in 1826. Young Pattie, with his father and several others, had been trapping beaver along the Gila River in present southwestern Arizona. After Indian thievery had cost them their pelts, the elder Pattie turned to copper mining, but James took to the trail. He followed the Gila west to its junction with the Colorado, then turned northeast to trace the big river up through the Grand Canyon, past the San Juan's mouth, and onward through hundreds of dangerous and laborious miles to the Continental Divide—an almost unbelievable exploit. Although the Pattie journal is so lacking in detail that most of the route cannot be ascertained, it appears probable that he and his companions followed the Colorado as nearly as they could. The crossing of the Divide was made in six days along a narrow buffalo trail which cut through "compact drifts of snow higher than a man on horseback" and which was obstructed by many dead animals. Shortly after crossing, Pattie came to a fork of the South Platte River not far from Long's Peak; this indicates that he must have found one of the passes near the Colorado River's head. After a northward excursion to the Big Horn or the Yellowstone, the men traveled south to the Rio Grande and thence to Santa Fe, where their skins were confiscated and they were jailed. Pattie's return to the Gila, his trapping voyage down the Colorado to its mouth, and eventual broken journey back to Cincinnati by way of San Diego and Mexico City complete the unparalleled saga of a dauntless adventurer and the first white man known to traverse the entire length of the Colorado. He was undoubtedly one among several Western

63

Slope pathfinders who learned a great deal about the river, but Pattie was the first to write of his experiences in the Rocky Mountain portion of its watershed.

Trail of the Upper Colorado

The infant Colorado emerges from the Granby Reservoir—hardly more than a brook—and begins at once its work of trenching the complex jumble of parallel and traverse ranges, plateau remnants, and intervening valleys which comprise the Colorado Rockies. Gathering volume and strength from the contributions of other mountain-born streams and rivers, it forms a series of gorges whose varied nature reflects the type of rocks which are penetrated. Today the river is closely followed by a highway throughout most of its length from the Granby outlet to near the Colorado-Utah border, and it has an inseparable companion in the Denver & Rio Rrande Western Railroad, which is obliged to pass through many tunnels in order to negotiate the steep, corrugated canyon walls. It is axiomatic that in mountainous or desert country, lines of communication follow the course of rivers; the map of Colorado state bears striking testimony to this fact.

In the late 1880's the fanciful notion of routing a continental railroad within the great lower canyons of the Colorado River was promulgated by a businessman named Frank M. Brown, who set himself up as president of the "Denver, Colorado Canyon and Pacific Railroad Corporation." Brown drove the first stake in Grand Junction, then proceeded to launch a de-luxe expedition (minus life-preservers) to survey the route. A member of his party was the eminent civil engineer, Robert Brewster Stanton, who took charge after the expedition had met with disastrous losses including the corporation's president and two other men, who drowned. Stanton tardily disbanded the expedition, still far

Torrent in the Desert

64

short of its goal. However, he organized a second survey which finally succeeded in reaching the Gulf of California after four laborious months on the river. His report of the survey indicated that the railroad was feasible both physically and economically, but it failed to attract sufficient capital. It is interesting to speculate as to the influence the railroad might have had upon Colorado River development, had this scheme materialized.

Upstream Tributaries

The streams and rivers which tumble down the Divide's western face to join the Colorado in its first 120 miles have physical features not unlike those of the main branch. Among the most beautiful white-water streams of this continent are those which empty directly into the river and its reservoirs from the steep mountain ravines—the Arapaho, East Inlet, Tonahutu, Onahu, and many others. The small rivers of this watershed were exploited for fur animals, panned for gold, then put to various domestic and commercial uses. Unlike the Green River, which traverses a very sparsely settled region, the Upper Colorado and its branches have for nearly a century provided the basis of livelihood for an increasing urban and rural population, now in excess of 80,000. The small communities that have grown up along the river here were established to supply the business needs of mining, grazing, and argricultural interests which developed in the neighboring valleys during the 1870's and '80's.

The Moffat Road; Tributary Development

Several towns owe their existence to the coming of the Moffat Railroad in 1905, along which they became shipping points for local produce. The Moffat road, planned to meet the demand for a more direct route from Denver to northwestern Colorado

From the Roof-tops of the Continent

65

and Salt Lake City, was laid from Denver westward over the Divide at Corona Pass, descending through the Fraser River Canyon and aligning its track with the Colorado River at Granby. When constructed, it was a local line which served the Yampa River valley, ending at Craig. Its builder had projected an extension to Salt Lake City via the lower Yampa valley and certain of the Green River canyons, but was unable to finance construction beyond Craig. In 1934 the Denver & Rio Grande connected with the Moffat line by way of the Dotsero cutoff to complete the direct transcontinental link, and later absorbed the Moffat into its system.

Rail communication was a great stimulus to the development of the entire upper Colorado basin, but the tributary streams themselves have played an even more important role in regional history than has the railroad. Fraser and Williams forks, which rise among the spectacular peaks of the Park Range, drop steeply from their granite heights to traverse the rolling foothills and treeless valleys which surround the Colorado River. The Fraser serves as guide to the transcontinental railroad and contributes from its headwaters to a transmountain diversion supplying the city of Denver via the Moffat tunnel. Williams Fork is now impounded so that its water may enter the Colorado through a regulating dam in replacement of water withdrawn by Denver from its own upper branches and those of the Blue River. Heretofore the Blue's water, stored in Green Mountain Reservoir, was used solely for replacement of the Adams Tunnel withdrawal from Grand Lake at the head of the Colorado. Under the new plan Blue River will add its contribution to the Denver city water system through 23-mile Harold D. Roberts tunnel, fourth and largest of the Denver diversion tunnels which pierce the Continental Divide. The power plant at the Green Mountain installation continues to supply hydro-electric power to drive the various pump-

Torrent in the Desert

66

ing stations in the complex network of water-use facilities on the Upper Colorado.

EARLY EXPLORATION IN THE UPPER COLORADO BASIN

The Blue River, in its untrammeled state, was distinguished as the locale of an abortive but fascinating Colorado River voyage, made in the same year as the first Powell expedition—1869. A self-styled explorer of the Colorado, the same Samuel Adams who had wangled Congressional commendation for duplicating Lieutenant Ives' 1858 trip up the lower reaches of the river, decided to try his hand at downstream travel. He went to Breckenridge, a mountain mining camp nearly two miles above sea level, and with ten recruits built four open rowboats in which they started down the Blue. In ten days they reached the Upper Colorado after a descent of 4,000 feet on or in the Blue River, having lost half of the boats, five men, and most of their provisions. The party pulled itself together and after a few days the remaining six members pushed off into the Colorado. Sixteen days later the boats were gone and three more men left the expedition. Doggedly the three die-hards built and wrecked, successively, four rafts. Finally, suffering from extreme exposure and starvation, they were "compelled to yield to the force of circumstances." Though the voyage lacked scientific merit, as a feat of intrepidity it has few equals.

CANYONS OF THE UPPER COLORADO

From its high snowbound birthplace the Colorado courses through Middle Park, one of the three great valleys which lie among the ridges of the central Colorado Rockies, then enters a varied series of gorges and canyons linked by valleys as it passes through a region of extremely complex topography. Large mountain streams draining the ranges to the south and White River

Plateau country to the north pour their silt-laden waters into the young river. Notable among the Upper Colorado's canyons are Gore and Glenwood Canyons. As the river saws its way through the foothills of the Gore Mountains, precipitous walls enclose a savage current lashed into thunderous rapids by a narrow boulder-strewn channel having the steepest gradient of the entire river —360 feet in five miles. Some fifty miles downstream, Glenwood Canyon with its steep banded cliffs is the site of a concrete dam and power plant which supply electricity to the city of Denver. In the two and one-half miles between dam and power plant the Colorado is a continuous rapid which boils furiously into a chaos of huge waves. In the Glenwood area two large tributaries join the Colorado—the Eagle and the Roaring Fork. These streams rise in the rugged Sawatch range and descend to the Colorado over shining runways which they have been grinding into the rocky headlands for millions of years—in all ways similar to that of the Colorado itself.

PLATEAU COUNTRY OF WESTERN COLORADO STATE

About a score of miles downstream from Glenwood Springs the red juniper-mantled hills recede from the river, and flat-topped land forms appear, signaling the river's emergence from the mountains into the plateau country. Western Colorado state consists of a series of great westward-dipping plateaus; Grand Mesa, White River, Yampa, Roan and Uncompahgre Plateaus comprise most of this system. Because of its arid climate and widespread breaking-up of the highlands by canyons, the region is sparsely populated except for railroad shipping centers and cultivated riverside valleys. Grand Mesa, one of the world's largest flat-topped mountains, rises to an altitude of 10,300 feet. Its hard basalt cap contains a great number of lakes and supports a national recreation area. Uncompahgre Plateau, south and west of Grand Mesa, is a notable exception to the rule that land forms are the result, rather than the cause, of watercourses. This 100-mile-long plateau has a core of granite covered by a thin layer of sedimentary rock. The formations are strikingly evident in the Colorado National Monument near Grand Junction, where the strata are exposed in high vertical cliffs. Here also are extensive fossil deposits containing incomplete dinosaur remains and petrified plant life. The rising of this plateau has deflected the Colorado River to the north, so that instead of passing through the center of this land mass, as it once did, the river now flows around the north end of the plateau. The dry, abandoned channel, known today as Unaweap Canyon, contains fifty miles of automobile road.

To the north of the Colorado River, the lofty table-top margins of immense White River Plateau may be glimpsed through side canyons and from the valley floor as far east as the mouth of Blue River and west of Rifle the light buff-and-gray face of the evergreen-topped Roan Cliffs appear. These cliffs, together with the "Book Cliffs" which form their lower terrace in many places, are the most evident and characteristic part of the Roan Plateau. They extend from this region westward along the Colorado's north bank until the river takes a more southerly course near the Utah border. The Roan and Book Cliffs continue westward across Utah, where they are breached by the Green River in Desolation and Gray Canyons, and remain visible for many miles northwestward along the Price River Valley, where extensive coal deposits are mined. The Roan Cliffs near Rifle are associated with a geologic formation which contains rich oil shales, and in western Colorado state a huge tract of the deposit, containing an estimated one trillion barrels of kerogen, has been placed under federal reserve. Successful experiments in recovery of shale oil forecast the

From the Roof=
tops of
the Continent

69

early development of a gigantic processing operation in Grand Valley. A fabulous "shale city" has been charted by graduate students in regional planning to extend for thirty miles along the Colorado River in Grand Valley, which will serve an estimated 350,000 persons in an urban complex ideally designed to suit regional features as well as human and industrial requirements. At present this transmutation is evidenced by pilot plants of the Bureau of Mines and certain oil companies, as well as distant laboratories where shale processing methods are under study.

The horizon south of the Colorado River is far more varied than its opposite on the north. The eroded margins of Battlement Mesa near Rifle and, farther west, of Grand Mesa, make irregular intrusions into the valley. Some of these appear as isolated promontories whose angular slopes are heavily mantled with dark sage. These promontories are to be the site of residential areas associated with the shale development. Mines, refineries, and other industries will be located opposite, in canyons and on bottoms north of the river. Below the mouth of silt-laden Roan Creek, which has its source high in plateau lands, the expansive floor of Grand Valley is disturbed by an intrusion of architecture-like buff cliffs enclosing the sluggish Colorado current. This canyon, named the Debeque, contains several coal mines and two water diversion structures; the latter, with their canal systems, supply irrigation water to the famed orchards of Grand Valley, which may be seen near the river for many miles.

Gunnison River; Black Canyon

The Gunnison River, which joins the Colorado opposite the city of Grand Junction, is an outstanding feature of Grand Valley and the largest of the Upper Colorado tributaries. its waters head in a far-flung segment of the Continental Divide in west central

70

Colorado State. It flows through terrain almost as varied as that which surrounds the Upper Colorado itself, from skyscraping granite peaks of the Divide to the plateau country surrounding Grand Valley. Its lower canyon separates Grand Mesa from the Uncompahgre Plateau to the west. The Black Canyon of the Gunnison is a prime example of the deep, precipitous gorge formed by a river as it emerges from a mountainous area. The steep gradient of the mountain river accelerates its downcutting and enables the grit-laden stream to chisel through rock much faster than horizontal erosion can keep pace; this results in the formation of a narrow, sheer-walled canyon as the river continues to cut headward. The Gunnison has carved a breathtaking chasm through beds of ancient dark granite, gneiss and schist, so that the spectator can peer straight down for an average 2,000 feet to the seething current. Throughout most of this canyon the river has no banks, only the slate-colored walls which rise unbroken to the canyon rim far above. It is difficult to realize that these forbidding narrows have been navigated by many river parties.

HUMAN DRAMA ALONG THE GUNNISON

Because of its favored location, the Gunnison River has a richer historical background than many of the upstream tributaries. An early fur trading fort was established during the 1830's by an infamous trapper and trader named Robidoux, near the junction of the Uncompahgre and Gunnison Rivers. At that time this land was the undisputed domain of the Utes, and for several years the fort flourished as a meeting place for white travelers and roving inhabitants of all colors. It suffered the common fate of beaver institutions, and had already disappeared by 1853, when Captain John Gunnison passed the site. Gunnison, a topographical engineer, was selected by the Secretary of War for command of a surveying party to explore one of four possible Pacific railway routes, this to follow the 38th parallel as nearly as practicable. Gunnison's party with a military escort set out from St. Louis over the Sante Fe Trail, crossed the mountains of southern Colorado and broached the Divide at Cochetopa Pass. Desscending northward into the valley, they came to the Gunnison River; this they called the "Grand," perhaps mistaking it for the Upper Colorado—then known as the Grand River. The party followed the Gunnison for 150 miles to its junction with the Colorado, where they again turned west on their long trek to California. Captain Gunnison lost his life on this expedition, and the river was later given his name in commemoration. The trail which he followed through Colorado state was one already well known to Indians and New Mexican traders; indeed, Cochetopa Pass bears the Ute name of the animal who discovered the passage long before the first human entered this mountain wilderness—the buffalo.

Torrent in the Desert

The Gunnison River also witnessed the enforced withdrawal of the Uncompahgre Utes from their tribal homeland following the White River uprising, "Colorado's last Indian war." The fourteen hundred dispossessed Utes, with their thousands of livestock moved sullenly down the Gunnison to the Colorado River, then along the latter for some distance enroute to their new lands in Utah. Almost before the last Indian had disappeared, the rich bottomlands of the Gunnison and its larger branches were staked by settlers, and dryfarming and cattle-raising commenced.

GRAND VALLEY

Grand Valley, which contains the Colorado River from above Rifle to near the Utah border, was little known until the late 1800's. White traders and trappers rarely passed that way, since

72

the plateau country to the west was Ute land and had little to offer them. However, interest in the rich bottomlands grew among white employees of the Indian agency and others who had visited the area, so that the expulsion of the Utes in 1881 was greeted with great jubilation and a wild scramble for the land. The confluence of the Gunnison and the Grand was recognized by the first eager land-seekers as a natural site for an important city, and plans had been formed so that civic development could begin as soon as the land was declared open to entry. Thus, the town of Grand Junction was laid out on the north bank of the Colorado River and projected into being almost overnight. Though cattle ranching was the original industry of Grand Valley, dryfarming with the use of Colorado River water soon began to encroach upon the range, and within a few years irrigation of the fertile valley had transformed it into one of the richest fruit- and produce-raising areas of the state. The Denver and Rio Grande railroad reached the town in 1882; this event brought trading, manufacturing, and culture to Grand Junction. With a population near 18,000, it is today the largest city in the state west of Boulder. The Colorado flows quietly near the foot of the Uncompahgre Plateau, pursuing its ageless career as sculptor of the land. No rapids mar its surface here. Now a mature river, it seems to be gathering strength for the herculean onslaught of the great canyons of Utah and Arizona.

From the Rooftops of the Continent

DOLORES RIVER

West of Fruita, where Grand Valley fades into the desert, the Colorado attaches itself more closely to the Uncompahgre Plateau, and begins to breach the foothills of this highland, creating a deep trough through the colorful rock beds of its margins. Approaching the isolated LaSal Mountain group, with its exquisitely pointed snowclad summits, the Colorado passes from the Uncompahgre fringe to penetrate the elevated northern base of these mountains. In the midst of a welter of painted canyons the river is joined by one sizeable tributary, the Dolores. This small river, called by Father Escalante "Rio de Nuestra Senora de los Dolores," traces a long and troublesome course from its origin north of Mesa Verde country to the Colorado River in Utah. Its historical distinction stems from the Escalante pilgrimage of 1776, when the redoubtable Franciscan and his party made their way along its course for a considerable distance in their search for a practicable route to the Pacific coast. They found the river banks greatly overgrown with thickets, and the Dolores ungratefully buried itself in many deep, impassable gorges. However, the party was obliged to stay within reach of it, since the location of water-holes was unknown and the only drinking water and pasturage available were afforded by the river. At times the men could proceed only by way of the stream bed, crossing and recrossing the rocky, treacherous channel, until at last they were unable to follow the river longer. Throughout most of its length the Dolores flows north and northwest through eroded plateau lands to join the Colorado near that unique assemblage of grotesque and beautiful forms in orange sandstone—the Arches National Monument. The Dolores lower channel is extremely diverse in appearance because of the broken terrain. Uranium has been found in high cliffs overlooking the river's mouth and elsewhere along its upstream branches.

Environs of Moab

Below the Dolores the Colorado enters a gorge of broken red cliffs and rich bottomlands where deep clefts in the walls reveal desert landscape beyond and occasional glimpses of the

74

12,000-foot LaSal peaks. Several ranches occupy the bottoms and "Fisher Towers," a group of natural spires, are an interesting feature of the area. A secondary road follows the river through this superb canyon. At its foot the Colorado is spanned by a highway bridge and the town of Moab has grown up in the cliff-bound valley which extends southward from the river. Settled by Mormon colonists a century ago, Moab developed slowly as a farming community at the edge of the desert which surrounds the LaSal Mountains. Discovery of oil, gas, and uranium in southeastern Utah has transformed the town into a bustling center of commercial enterprise. Motorboats now ply the Colorado, on business as well as pleasure, from Moab docks.

DEAD HORSE POINT

Resuming its canyon-wise career below the cleft at Moab, the river takes a winding course among tall, colorful bluffs, traversing a gorge very similar in plan and character to the Labyrinth of the Green River. The same rock layers appear, the gradient is of like degree—indeed, these converging channels may be regarded as actual twins. A score of miles above the junction, the Colorado has carved a "gooseneck" from the thick beds of rock that it has penetrated. Towering 2,000 feet above this bend is a promontory of the Junction Plateau which many years ago was used as a natural corral by local cowboys. According to the story, about fifty wild mustangs perished of thirst on this point because they could not find their way back to mainland across the narrow neck. The panorama viewed from the southern tip of Dead Horse Point is unquestionably the most handsome on the Upper Colorado. It extends to the horizon in three directions, embracing a hundred miles of contorted desert landscape with its weird buttes and step-like terraces that surround the river like a great amphi-

75

theater. This fantastic mosaic with its startling contrasts of shape and color is surmounted by the snow-capped peaks of the LaSal, Abajo, and Henry Mountains.

THE "NEEDLES"

Across the Colorado from the Junction plateau and extending some distance to the south lies another region of scenic amazement so characteristic of the weathered land margins which enclose the river—known as the "Needles." Here long rows, clusters, and pyramids of stone pinnacles rise from the sandy fill of the desert floor. Tall and slender, squat or gnarled—like giant mushrooms, Grecian urns, or temple colonnades of banded red and white sandstone—these whimsical forms delight the observer with their endless variety of proportion, color, and arrangement. The "Needles" spread far into the desert above and below the confluence of the Green and the Colorado, gradually losing themselves among the outstretched fingers of Dark Canyon Plateau, which forms the broad pedestal of Elk Ridge and the Abajo Mountains. This plateau and its partner to the north, Standing Rock Plateau, confine the Colorado within that uneasy corridor, Cataract Canyon.

Torrent in the Desert

The Source

*The Never-Summer Mountains
and Kawuneeche Valley*

*Grand Lake and the
Front Range*

Arapaho Creek
(facing page)

Powerhouse on the Blue River

Sheephorn Creek

Below Gore Canyon

*The Plateaus begin in
Western Colorado*

The Eagle River

Shoshone Dam

The Colorado skirts the Roan Cliffs

Glenwood Springs, at the
Mouth of Roaring Fork

Independence Rock, Colorado
National Monument

Black Cany
of the
Gunnison

The Dolores River

*LaSal Mountains
above the
Colorado*

Bluffs near Moab, Utah

The Delicate Arch
(facing page)

At Dead Horse Point

Evening Shower,
Dead Horse Point

*The LaSals from Dead
Horse Point*

*Stone Terraces
at Sunset*

*Monument Canyon from
the White Rim*

The Loop

*Indian Creek feeds Silt
to the Colorado*

The Needles Country

Within the Needles Labyrinth
(facing page)

Chapter 3

Down the Plateau
Province

It seems appropriate to think

of the Junction as that point where the two mountain-born parental forks of the Colorado lose their identity in the genesis of a river whose character is distinct from all those which formed it. Here begins the career of a tawny giant who shoulders his way through a land of great tilted blocks and leaves a yawning chasm in his wake.

THE CATARACT

From the beginning of Cataract Canyon, a few miles below the Junction, the Colorado passes through an almost unbroken chain of savage rapids between the serrated cliffs and great piles of debris which extend for forty miles southwest to Millecrag Bend. Nicknamed the "Graveyard of the Colorado," Cataract has claimed the lives of many ill-prepared or unlucky boatmen, and ranks with the Grand Canyon in difficulty of navigation. Though this canyon lacks the classical beauty of Glen Canyon and the color of Lodore, those who have braved its furious waters claim for it a supremacy based on its dynamics. Major Powell was captivated by the violence of Cataract, and wrote in poetic terms of its rapids. Because of the great number of line portages, boat repairs, and the extreme difficulty of passage, his boats averaged only about two miles a day in this canyon.

Down
the Plateau
Province

103

The essence of Cataract is most beautifully expressed in the words of Ellsworth Kolb as he witnessed his brother Emery piloting the "Edith" through Dark Canyon rapid during their 1911 photographic survey:

"I saw the gloom of the great gorge, and the towering, sinister shafts of rock, weakened with cracks, waiting for the moment that would send them crashing to the bottom. I saw the mad, wild water hurled at the curving wall. Jagged rocks, like the bared fangs of some dream-monster, appeared now and then in the leaping, tumbling waves. Then down toward the turmoil—dwarfed to nothingness by the magnitude of the walls—sped the tiny shell-like boat . . . The oar-blades were tipped high to avoid loss in the first comber; then the boat was buried in the foam, and staggered through on the other side. It was buffeted here and there, now covered with a ton of water, now topping a ten-foot wave . . . the oarsmen shot in his oars for two quick strokes, to straighten the boat with the current or dodge a threatening boulder; then covered by lifting his oars and ducking his head as a brown flood rolled over him. Time and again the manoeuvre was repeated . . . by some sort of a system, undoubtedly aided many times by good luck, the man and his boat won to land."*

THE "DIRTY DEVIL"

As the thunder of Cataract dies in the tailwater of U-shaped Millecrag, the Colorado receives a very silty and sulfurous contribution from a small river christened the "Dirty Devil's Creek" by Major Powell. This stream, whose origins are far away among

*Quoted by permission of the Macmillan Company from E. L. Kolb: "Through the Grand Canyon from Wyoming to Mexico," copyright 1914.

the complex of plateaus north and west of the Henry Mountains, is formed by the union of the Muddy and Fremont Rivers. The Fremont, whose name is often applied to the main stream, traverses a thinly settled farming and grazing area in its first seventy-five miles. The Muddy drains an area peopled only by lizards and rockhunters before it enters the forsaken sandstone wilderness of Green River Desert, where the "Dirty Devil" keeps its lonely rendezvous with the big river.

THE LANDING AT HITE

A small settlement occupies the north bank of the Colorado at the mouth of Trachyte Creek, eight miles downstream from the Dirty Devil. Its present name is that of a hermit prospector, Cass Hite, who lived there from 1883 until 1898. When the discovery of gold in Glen Canyon brought swarms of would-be prospectors to the Colorado, he moved downstream to Ticaboo Creek, where he spent the remainder of his life. In his declining years he enjoyed an unusual friendship with young Bert Loper, who also worked a small placer mine, lived alone and read voraciously in his cabin beside the Colorado, a short distance upstream at the mouth of Red Canyon. After Cass' death, Loper returned to civilization and soon began his spectacular career as Colorado riverman and guide.

A miner's postoffice and supply station was set up at Hite in the '90's and the settlement continued in existence after the gold fever subsided. The river crossing to White Canyon, long known to Indians and to early white travelers, who called it "Dandy's Crossing," became part of a Mormon wagon route between Bluff settlement on the San Juan River and communities in central Utah.

Principal activity now centers about the ferry, which still carries travelers across the river. The village of White Canyon, directly opposite Hite, is connected by road with Blanding and

105

other towns of southeastern Utah. In recent years Hite has served as the embarkation point of many Colorado River boat expeditions in Glen Canyon, which extends from the Dirty Devil River downstream for nearly 200 miles to the head of Marble Canyon.

GLEN CANYON

This long, unique gorge was epithetically divided by Major Powell into Mound Canyon and Monument Canyon (respectively above and below the San Juan's mouth), according to the principal erosion forms in these sections. The smooth-domed salmon-pink sandstone which typifies Glen Canyon makes its appearance some distance below Hite as the cap layer of the broken orange-red cliffs which line the channel. Many mound-like prominences stud the bench here, but as the pink stone is exposed to its maximum depth of 1,200 feet, rounded monument-like peaks replace the mounds. This type of sandstone has made possible the formation of the many beautiful alcoved side canyons or "glens" which suggested the naming of this area to Powell. The "Music Temple" is the most elaborate of these exquisite alcoves; within its great curving dome are clear pools of water, murals of moss and fern, many flowering plants and small trees—contrasting the clean-swept lines of the bare stone which surrounds this crypt-like oasis. The carved inscriptions of Powell's boatmen and other early visitors may still be seen on a rock face within the Temple.

An interesting phenomenon of nature may be observed in various of the Colorado canyons—perhaps best in the Glen, where vertical monolithic walls rise as high as a thousand feet from water level. Following a cloudburst, which frequently occurs in summer, a great volume of rain water drains from the smooth stone bench through shallow channels to the canyon rim, where it plunges downward in a beautiful cascade. Up and down the river dozens of these fleeting waterfalls delight the fortunate spectator.

Side canyons reaching back into the benchlands on both sides of Glen Canyon afford some of the most unusual and provocative features of the entire Colorado watershed. At the mouth of Red Canyon, not far below Hite, are still to be seen the remnants of the first recorded prehistoric site in Glen Canyon, discovered by members of Major Powell's 1869 river party. A few minutes' walk from this much-visited ruin stands a century-old log cabin that is said to have been built by an outlaw. Now vacant but still well preserved, this cabin was claimed as home by Bert Loper for several years before he set out to conquer the Colorado. This indomitable explorer not only passed through all of the major gorges of the Green and the Colorado several times, but ran his boat through certain canyons of the Upper Colorado and the Gunnison, as well as some little-known portions of the Green above the traditional launching point at Green River City, Wyoming. He completed his conquest of the Colorado River with a cruise from Needles to the Gulf of California, and ended his saga in Marble Canyon a few days before his eightieth birthday, still at the oars.

Directly south of the Henry Mountains a small stream known as Hall's Creek descends to the river through a deep, narrow opening in the cliffs. A jeep trail still travels the route of 19th-century travelers who ferried across the Colorado here, on their way to the San Juan River Mormon settlements. In 1922 this crossing was the embarkation point of a little-known Colorado River expedition whose distinguished personnel examined eight possible damsites in Glen Canyon just prior to their participation in the Santa Fe conference which framed the Colorado River Compact. The contribution of Dr. John Widtsoe in safeguarding Upper Basin rights at this conference is rivaled in value by his inspired journal of the Glen Canyon expedition. He noted with great keeness and humili-

Down
the Plateau
Province

ty, not only the daily experiences of his party on the river, but the brilliant immensity of a superb canyon.

Another of the Glen's small tributaries, called Lake Canyon, is an outstanding example of the many fissures cut into the deep pink sandstone bluffs by perennial streamlets. Its course is a steep, winding groove filled with delightful surprises which include waterfalls, a small seasonal lake, Indian ruins and earlier sites, as well as a perfect grotto. Lake Canyon has long been a favorite side trip for Colorado River parties, but will be largely submerged by rising water of the Glen Canyon reservoir.

"Hole in the Rock," a narrow cleft between 1400-foot cliffs overlooking the Colorado, is the site of one of those heroic acts of labor and suffering which characterize early Mormon colonization in Utah. In 1879 seventy families of pioneers from Utah's "Dixie" came to this place, which had been selected after a hasty survey, and camped for several months while their men chiseled, blasted, and built this crevice into a breakneck wagon road down to the river. The colonists then ferried the wagons across the Colorado, forcing their animals to swim, and proceeded to hack out a trail of agony through more than a hundred miles of scorched and rockbound wilderness to establish the Bluff settlement on the San Juan River. The roadway through the "Hole" was so dangerous and difficult that it was used by wagons for less than two years. As it stands today, the upper half of the fissure is choked with fallen boulders and all trace of the roadbed has disappeared except for some drill holes, bits of masonry and chiseling. To travel the old route in either direction requires a fairly strenuous climb.

Below the San Juan's mouth is the semi-concealed entrance to one of the great scenic wonders of the world. Aztec and Bridge Creeks issue from the foot of Navajo Mountain, that inscrutable dome of gray-blue which dominates the desert scene for a hundred miles round. These small crystal brooks have etched their way through the broken pedestal of this mountain, reaching down into the very foundations which form the wall of Glen Canyon. Within the deep gorge of Bridge Creek, a short distance above its junction with Aztec Creek and five miles from the Colorado, stands the incomparable Rainbow Bridge. This grandest of all natural arches was unknown at the time of the Powell surveys; it was not seen by white men until 1909, when a Paiute Indian led Douglass, Cummings, and Wetherill to the wonder. Revered by the Indians as their "Nonnezoshi," and set aside as a national monument in 1910, it is to be materially altered by the Glen Canyon project. Though the 300-foot span itself is above maximum water level, Forbidding and Bridge Canyons will largely disappear under the waters of Lake Powell and access to the Bridge via the Colorado will be subject to water level fluctuation.

Elsewhere in Glen Canyon are relics of mining machinery which remind us of still-untouched deposits locked within these canyon walls; fords and campsites where Indians, settlers, prospectors, and all manner of human flotsam crossed the river or dwelt for a time on its banks; ruins and cliff writings of prehistoric cultures, and a place where Father Escalante found a crossing of the Colorado after desperate search in his return to Santa Fe. If all this were not enough, one finds that branches of the spectacular Escalante River canyon, which cuts the long basin between the Straight Cliffs and Waterpocket Fold, contain natural bridges of rare beauty, as well as numerous prehistoric human habitations. Under the auspices of the National Park Service, comprehensive survey and salvage excavations have been carried out by learned institutions in Glen Canyon and on the lower San Juan to preserve as much as possible of the scientific and cultural values of the areas to be flooded, as provided for by the federal Antiquity Act.

Down
the Plateau
Province

109

The name of Escalante has been given to several localities within the Colorado Basin, most of which were never visited by the Padre. In 1775 the Franciscan Velez de Escalante was ordered by the governor of New Mexico to prepare a report on a communication route between Santa Fe and New Spanish settlements on the California coast. Accordingly, the friar collected what information he could from his own and Father Garces' travels, and on July 29, 1776, began his fabled wilderness expedition. The exploration party of nine included, besides Velez, his superior Father Dominguez and several other persons of distinction, as well as guides and helpers; they were accompanied by a herd of cattle and numerous horses and mules to provide for their anticipated needs.

Torrent in the Desert

Instead of the obvious course south and westward along the Gila River valley, because of known Indian resistance there a more roundabout route was chosen which led northward, skirting the San Juan Mountains and reaching the Upper Colorado by way of the Dolores, Uncompahgre, and Gunnison Rivers. As far as the Uncompahgre Plateau most of the trail was known to the traders in the party. From this point onward the Padre moved in strange territory, guided part of the way by Indians whom he engaged en route, but during most of the journey merely by his nose and verbal directions he had received from natives in some distant place. The party made its first crossing of the Colorado below the present town of Grand Valley in western Colorado state, fording the rocky channel in water which "reached above the shoulder blades of the animals." From here they traveled northwest over the Roan Plateau, crossed the Green River seven times within the Uinta Basin, and continued westward over the Wasatch divide to an Indian settlement on the shore of Utah Lake, near modern Provo. Having accomplished the conversion of these people, Escalante pushed on through the mountainous center of Utah state, following the long valleys that trend southwestward along the great faults. By October, winter had begun on the Utah highlands; this was an important factor in the Father's decision not to go on to Monterey, but rather to seek the best return to Santa Fe.

They could not, of course, go directly toward this destination, but had to follow the topography in a land of massive cliffs and impassable canyons. After many long, costly detours, they reached the Colorado River and began eight days of search for the crossing of which they had been told by natives. The men lived on seeds and horse meat as they zigzagged along the precipitous north rim of Glen Canyon. On November 7 the ford was located, and the party successfully crossed the Colorado for the second and last time. Their exit from the canyon took them southward over the desert of northern Arizona to the Hopi towns, perched on the tops of high mesas, where they made friends but no converts. The party then hurried on as fast as their tired horses could go to Escalante's headquarters at Zuni, near the present Arizona-New Mexico border. A few weeks later Velez completed the 2000-mile cycle with his return to Santa Fe. His faithfully kept diary, like those of the Powell boatmen, has given the world a lucid colorful account of a notable exploration in the language of a warm-blooded protagonist.

SAN JUAN RIVER

The San Juan River approaches the Colorado through a gorge renowned for its contortions; in the "goosenecks" near the town of Mexican Hat, the meanders are so convoluted that several loops are separated by only a wafer-thin partition of stone. This river, which rises in the volcanic San Juan Mountains of southwestern Colorado state, is so seasonal that it sometimes carries as much

Down
the Plateau
Province

water as the Colorado during spring run-off, yet often is nearly dry a few weeks later because of irrigation withdrawals, evaporation, and soil drainage in the long journey across southern Utah. A large earth-fill Bureau of Reclamation dam, known as the Navajo, is under construction in the New Mexico segment of the river, a part of the Colorado Basin development program.

The original white settlement on the San Juan River was that established at Bluff in 1880 by Mormon pioneers who survived the terrible trek east from "Hole in the Rock." Even today, tiny Mexican Hat is the only other riverside town west of the Colorado state boundary, though a number of Indians live in side canyons and bottoms.

In the deep canyon country surrounding the San Juan are many superlative archaeologic sites. Incident to Charles Bernheimer's exploration of the immense, corrugated "rock jumble" on all sides of Navajo Mountain, scores of cliff ruins and other prehistoric sites, many of the early Basketmaker period, were discovered. The large elaborate structures at Keet Seel, Betatakin, and Inscription House, of later date, also are located in branches of this canyon system. Hovenweep National Monument in southeastern Utah contains four outstanding groups of prehistoric cliffside dwellings and towers. Perhaps best known of all are the rich treasures of well-preserved antiquity at Mesa Verde and Canyon de Chelly, which rank among our most valuable documents of life in America before the coming of Europeans.

PLATEAUS OF SOUTHERN UTAH

The bewildering variety of canyon architecture found in and about Glen Canyon has resulted from the action of the Colorado drainage system upon the edges of the plateaus which end at the river—the lofty Kaiparowitz, the Rainbow and Paria Plateaus. A

112

discussion of Glen Canyon must include also mention of the great upper tier of high plateaus that face the Colorado across southern Utah, at a distance of 80 to 100 miles from the river, and which provide water to all of its northern tributaries from the Dirty Devil to the Virgin River. It is thought that the Fishlake, Aquarius, Paunsaugunt, Markagunt, and Pine Valley plateaus once formed a continuous surface which has been much broken through faulting and erosion. Since these blocks have become differentiated, their erosion has occurred more in the horizontal than in the vertical plane, so that the faces exposed by earth movements have worn away in successive terraces. Brilliant examples of this pattern are the Pink Cliffs at Bryce Canyon, the White Cliffs at Zion Canyon, the Vermillion Cliffs along the Colorado at the head of Marble Canyon. These three terraces may be seen in striking apposition from U.S. Highway 89A as it crosses Kaibab Plateau's north rim. The distant plateau lands exert an influence upon the Glen Canyon through their contribution of water and their role in tributary erosion. Evidence of the processes which formed this majestic gorge is more striking here than else where in the Colorado watershed; every side canyon, every alcove and wash has its peculiar beauty, and each perennial stream creates its own emerald paradise within this vast stone wilderness.

The native qualities of Glen Canyon are to be drastically altered by the aforementioned 700-foot Bureau of Reclamation dam, which will impound the waters of the Colorado as far upstream as Cataract Canyon. The project is designed to provide key regulation of river flow, to trap silt which would otherwise accumulate in Lake Mead, and to generate additional power for Colorado Basin users. Its reservoir, Lake Powell, will have an 1800-mile shoreline; this is to be administered by the National Park Service as a public recreation area. The Glen Canyon high-

Down the Plateau Province

113

way bridge, completed very early in the dam construction, is the highest single-arch steel bridge in the world.

Lee's Ferry; Marble Canyon

One of the important crossings of the Middle Colorado is at Lee's Ferry, Arizona. Here the small Paria River, which rises at the base of Bryce Canyon, has ploughed its way through Paria Plateau's east rim to join the Colorado. At its mouth the renegade Mormon John D. Lee built a fort and settled part of his large family two years before his capture. He operated a ferry at this already-established river crossing, which continued in use from 1873 until the Navajo Bridge was built in 1929. Today only the crumbling remnants of the stone fort and a U.S. Geological Survey river-gauging station mark the old site. It is of interest that Lee's first ferryboat was the "Nellie Powell," abandoned at the Paria's mouth by the second Powell survey.

Lee's Ferry is one of a dozen places in the Colorado vicinity which are inseparably linked with the name Jacob Hamblin. A Mormon convert who came west to Salt Lake City with the first wave of emigrants, he dedicated himself to the career of missionary, guide, explorer, interpreter, and elite peacemaker among the Indians of Utah and Arizona. On the one hand, he strove unceasingly to adjust relations between red and white during the troublesome years when Indian tribes were being dispossessed of their lands by the encroachment of white settlements. On the other, he gave unsparingly of his effort to the pioneering tasks which made that encroachment possible. The demands of Hamblin's unusual occupation took him across the Colorado countless times. The first crossings were made at the Ute Ford, now known as Crossing of the Father's, and at the mouth of Paria Creek (later Lee's Ferry); these were occasioned by the earliest of seven missions to the Hopi people east of Grand Canyon. For the fourth mission he sought out a longer but less dangerous route which crossed the Colorado nearly 300 miles downstream, below Granite Gorge. Here he laid the groundwork for a wagon road and ferry, as he did at the Paria crossing. Between these tasks and his Indian troubleshooting, Hamblin found time to explore much of the canyon country, guide emigrant bands through dangerous territory, work with Major Powell in preparation for his 1872 river survey, build homes and manage a grazing enterprise.

Though the typical Glen features disappear some miles above Lee's Ferry, this point is usually considered the foot of Glen Canyon and the head of Marble Canyon. Here the red cliffs begin to recede from the river banks to make way for a comparatively level valley, the Marble Platform. This shelf expands south and west to include most of the area bounded by the Kaibab Plateau, Vermillion Cliffs, Echo Cliffs, and the Little Colorado River, whose deep winding course is invisible from the desert floor except at very close range. Above Marble Canyon's west rim looms the escarpment of Kaibab Plateau. As the gorge approaches Grand Canyon to the south, this steep Kaibab pedestal converges with the canyon rim and increasingly shows the erosion forms which typify the Grand. Isolated buttes appear in the vicinity of the Little Colorado junction. An unusual type of human visitation to this area deserves mention. Archaeologists have recently located an obscure trail leading to a massive deposit of salt, near the mouth of the Little Colorado. Certain of the Hopis have, for untold years, made ceremonial trips here to gather salt for their people. No salt mine could have a more unique or difficult locale.

THE GRAND CANYON

In passing the Little Colorado's mouth, which is more often

Down the Plateau Province

115

dry than wet, the big river crosses the threshhold of a canyon that is more than a canyon—one which transcends its physical nature to enter the realm of immortality. During the four centuries since discovery of the Grand Canyon by Lopez de Cardenas, leader of a Coronado detachment, innumerable attempts have been made to crystallize into language the impact of its vast, ethereal drama on human sensibilities. Few have succeeded. In the words of John Van Dyke, "The great chasm cannot be successfully exploited commercially or artistically . . . it is too big for one to do more than creep along the rim and wonder over it." A contrasting view was expressed by James Pattie, who faced the stark problem of survival as he traversed the South Rim, without water but in full sight of the Colorado River. He complained bitterly of "these horrid mountains which so cage it up . . .", making access to the stream a practical impossibility for men.

Grand Canyon vaunts a challenge to all who seek to penetrate it by visual, photographic, or pedestrian approach. For that small fraternity of men who undertook the conquest by way of the Colorado itself during the first half-century of its navigation history, the challenge became a tangible menace, unremitting and pitiless. Major John W. Powell, whose 1869 and '71 expeditions were the first known successful boat runs through the Canyon, was followed by other boatmen who came to survey, to make pictures, or simply to seek high adventure, some came more than once. Of these river pioneers Major Powell and Utah's Bert Loper are the most widely known. The Kolb brothers recorded the Colorado on film in a remarkably personal way and made Grand Canyon their livelihood. Other names—Stanton, Flavell, Monett, Russell—also are identified with successful conquests of Granite Gorge in the primitive days of riverboating. Credit for the success of many later expeditions is due Nathan Galloway, a trapper from

Torrent in the Desert

Richfield, Utah, who knew the Green and Colorado River systems as did no other man. Galloway introduced the stern-first technic and a special boat design for shooting rapids which became the standard for decades. This man was an unsung figure who went about his extraordinary business without fanfare. However, the wealthy sportsman from Ohio, Julius Stone—whom Galloway piloted through all the great canyons of the Green and the Colorado in 1909—photographed and published the most complete single exposition of them which exists even today.

The Spanish explorers, scouts, trappers, and government surveyors came, saw, and went away. Many of them wrote about the Canyon. However, it did not attract settlers until comparatively few decades ago. The Coconino Plateau, like its counterpart, the Kaibab, was extensively used for cattle and sheep range by Arizona ranchers long before the Santa Fe railroad was extended west from Winslow. With this development and the simultaneous discovery of rich mineral deposits in the Canyon, the great chasm began to draw attention.

In 1883 the tourist era opened with the first recorded sightseeing visit by Edward E. Ayer, a Chicago businessman who had built a sawmill in Flagstaff. The ever-increasing procession visitors who followed Ayer stimulated the development of trails and living facilities by the Canyon's only white residents—the mining prospectors. The best known of these was Captain John Hance. In the early '80's he had established a homestead and built a log cabin, the first structure on the South Rim, six miles east of present Grand Canyon Village. From his cabin he constructed a trail down the crumbling cliffs to his copper and asbestos claims, deep within the canyon. Early tourists began to use his trail for access to the inner gorge, and Hance initiated a summer guide and host service for the adventuresome spirits who came to the South Rim

Down
the Plateau
Province

117

in the 1880's. More than half of his early visitors had traveled from foreign countries, and many were distinguished professionals. Contemporaries of Hance were Pete Berry and Niles Cameron, who together built the original Bright Angel trail over a faint Indian trace descending to their claims at Indian Gardens on the Tonto Rim, and charged visitors a toll for its use. This trail passed through the hands of other owners and finally was obtained by the National Park Service in 1928.

By 1895 a main stageline brought travelers to the South Rim from Flagstaff, and various accommodations were available—some in the most unlikely places, as the mouth of Diamond Creek, at the end of a long primitive wagon road which led from the top of Hualpai Plateau to the Colorado's banks thousands of feet below. W. W. Bass' "camp" was built at the head of another canyon access trail 25 miles west of the Bright Angel route. Bass developed his trail over an old Indian footpath, established a low-water ferry and a cableway across the Colorado at its lower end, and operated a stageline from his camp to the town of Williams. Other improved trails which led down into the Canyon during pioneering days were the Grandview, Tanner, Boucher, Hermit, and Old trails, as well as the Nankoweap built by Major Powell on the North Rim. Of all these early routes the only one now maintained by the Park Service is the remodeled Bright Angel, which connects by a riverside link to the modern canyon-spanning Kaibab Trail.

Developments on the North Rim were somewhat slower by comparison. The Mormons had brought their herds to the Kaibab forest in the 1850's, and cattle grazing continued to be the principal enterprise, along with trapping, hunting, and prospecting, until the National Park was created in 1919. Early Grand Canyon guide Dave Rust set up a camp at the mouth of Bright Angel Creek where tourists were accommodated for several years. This establishment was served by a trail from the North Rim, forerunner of the present Kaibab route. The old campsite was taken over in 1921 by the Sante Fe-Harvey interests, which built Phantom Ranch there. The Kaibab Trail, rim access roads, and tourist facilities have been more recent accomplishments of the National Park Service and its concessionnaires.

The Grand Canyon affords one of the earth's prime examples of stream erosion. In its 217 miles the Colorado River has exposed a nearly complete geologic section ranging from the Kaibab limestone of Permian age (about 200 million years) at the canyon's rim, downward thousands of feet to the metamorphic Archeozoic rock of the inner gorge, some of the oldest known to geologists—perhaps two billion years old. This astounding chasm was formed by running water which continued in its course while the region around it was slowly elevated. The horizontal attitude of the upper rock layers, together with softness of some and hardness of others, has resulted in the creation of architecture-like forms in alternating cliffs and slopes. Despite vertical displacement between North and South Rims, the same layers may be easily identified in both. The fantastically varied rock forms seen on every hand have evolved through action of streamlets that tumble down the canyon walls, coupled with wind, heat, and frost. The river carries one-half to one million tons of silt past any point in Grand Canyon every 24 hours, so it is easy to comprehend the removal of the land mass which once filled this great gulf.

Plant and animal life in the Canyon represent four distinct climatic zones which result from the extreme range in altitude between river level and the outer rims. Thus it is possible to descend within a few hours from Boreal forests of whispering conifers to the spiny cactus and delicate mesquite of the lower Sonoran zone. For those who remain on the canyon rim, enchantment lies

Down
the Plateau
Province

119

in the constantly changing atmosphere and light conditions peculiar to this "inverted mountain range," playing upon the castellated slopes, now highlighting the battlements with gold, now plunging the depths into purple gloom, projecting that endless pageant of color and form which is Grand Canyon.

HAVASUPAI

The hundreds of Indian ruins found among the canyon walls of the Colorado River are easily accepted as part of the general antiquity. It is, however, surprising to learn that in the very bowels of the Grand Canyon system an agrarian community has persisted for centuries with little basic change until very recent times. The 3,000-foot walls of Havasu Canyon were first penetrated by white man in 1775. This man was Father Garces, a sort of ecclesiastical Daniel Boone of the Southwest, who is also credited with naming the Colorado. An inveterate crusader, he was driven by a desire to explore new territory, as well as to save the souls of heathen. It was on his fifth "entrada" or exploratory mission that he made his way down the near-vertical cliff trail into this tiny, hidden retreat of the Havasupai tribe. He found willing converts among the pleasant natives, and resumed his journey rejoicing that he had secured their souls to redemption.

The Havasupais today are still a good-natured, easy-going people whose ways have not been greatly influenced by white men's religions. Only a fraction of the tribe can find space to live in their canyon paradise; the others have found homes and livelihoods elsewhere, in towns and on homesteads in Arizona and California. Those who remain in Supai do not lead an abundant life; there are still too many inhabitants for the present economy. Within the red-walled ancestral valley fruits and vegetables are raised in the bright sand by irrigation methods; it is said

Torrent in the Desert

120

that cultivation of fruit trees was introduced by John D. Lee, who lived there for several years as a fugitive following the massacre at Mountain Meadows and before he established the fort at Lee's Ferry in Marble Canyon. Horses are the principal index of prosperity in Supai, as well as the prevalent source of money income.

The basis of all life here is the blue-green water of beautiful Havasu River. This remarkable stream, whose English name is Cataract Creek, wells up from the bedrock of the canyon a mile or so above the village and descends 1,400 feet to its junction with the Colorado. Its water is so heavily laden with calcium carbonate that the mineral is deposited in crystalline form called "travertine" upon any obstruction, most notably at places where there is a break in the river bed. Thus it forms "curtains" which hang from the top of falls, and builds up in terraces below. Striking examples of travertine are seen at the three principal falls of this canyon— Navajo, Havasu, and Mooney.

Quite naturally the Havasu is subject to flash flood, and "washouts" are a common occurrence. In 1910 a severe winter flood inundated the entire valley and drove the Indians onto the upper terrace, from which they would not descend for many years, despite strong persuasive action by the Indian Service. Stone cairns and storage granaries may still be seen on this shelf, remnants of former occupancy. The handsome falls also may be viewed from this terrace, though the inner canyon trail is most used by visitors.

THE GRAND CANYON MONUMENT

A few miles below the mouth of Havasu River the National Park ends and Grand Canyon National Monument begins. This tract, which extends for thirty miles on the north side of the Colorado and a short segment of the south rim, is almost entirely un-developed for public use, though it possesses impressive scenic and recreational values. Here the architectural formula is altered; instead of the long terraces which descend gradually from widely separated rims to the 1,500-foot inner gorge, as seen in the National Park, here one finds a steep drop of a thousand feet from canyon rim to a broad platform which spreads inward to the brink of the plunging 3,000-foot walls of the river channel. Thus the Colorado is viewed from directly above, instead of from a vantage point several miles distant. Forested volcanic peaks rise high above the canyon walls, and near Toroweap Point numerous "recent" lava flows have reached down into the gorge. One of these obstructed the river for a time, and its remnants are yet the cause of the most dangerous rapids on the Colorado—Lava Falls.

Torrent in the Desert

LOWER GRANITE GORGE

From the western boundary of the National Monument, the Colorado's rims are included within the enormous Lake Mead Recreation Area, a federal preserve. In this area the lower Grand Canyon is invaded by the blue waters of Lake Mead. Quartermaster Viewpoint on the south rim is one of a few points where the river gorge is accessible by road.

Future visitors to this locality will witness the erection of a 740-foot power dam, loftier than Hoover and Glen Canyon Dams, now planned for the site at Bridge Canyon. This dam, still controversial, may be the initial construction of a Grand Canyon power development that will include another high dam in Marble Gorge and a 45-mile tunnel which will carry most of the Colorado flow under the Kaibab plateau to a power plant near the mouth of Kanab Creek.

122

Dark Canyon Rapid,
Cataract Canyon

Evening Landing, Cataract Canyon

At North Wash, Near Hite

The Fremont River

*The Old Chaffin
Ferry at Hite*

Loper's Cabin,
Glen Canyon

Aftermath of a Cloudburst
(facing page)

Flood at Ticaboo Creek

Gathering Storm over
Glen Canyon

Ruin in Lake Canyon

Canyon of the Escalante River

Evening in Glen Canyon

Chiseled Steps at
"Hole-in-the-Rock"

Road to Bluff, Utah

Wagon Road,
"Hole-in-the-Rock"

*Goosenecks of the
San Juan River*

Music Temple

Glen Canyon Near Aztec Creek

Forbidding Canyon

*Swimming Pool in
Aztec Canyon*

Rainbow Bridge

The Keyhole, Glen Canyon

"Nonnezoshi"

The Crossing of the Fathers

Flood at Kane Creek

"Labyrinth", a Glen Canyon Tributary

Sentinel
Rock

Glen Canyon Dam,
Early Construction

Glen Canyon Dam,
October, 1962

Bryce Canyon

Lee's Fort
(facing page)

*The Colorado and
Marble Platform*

*Navajo Bridge
(facing page)*

Cataract Boats Entering
Marble Canyon

The Gorge of the
Little Colorado

From Point Imperial

North Rim View

Desert View

From Cape Royal

From the Old Hermit Trail

Kaibab Bridge

Spring on the Tonto Platform

Kanab Creek

*Canyon
Home
of the
Havasupai*

*Havasu
Falls*

In Granite Gorge

Toroweap

Lava Falls

Chapter 4

Dams, Dusty Water, and Green Paradise

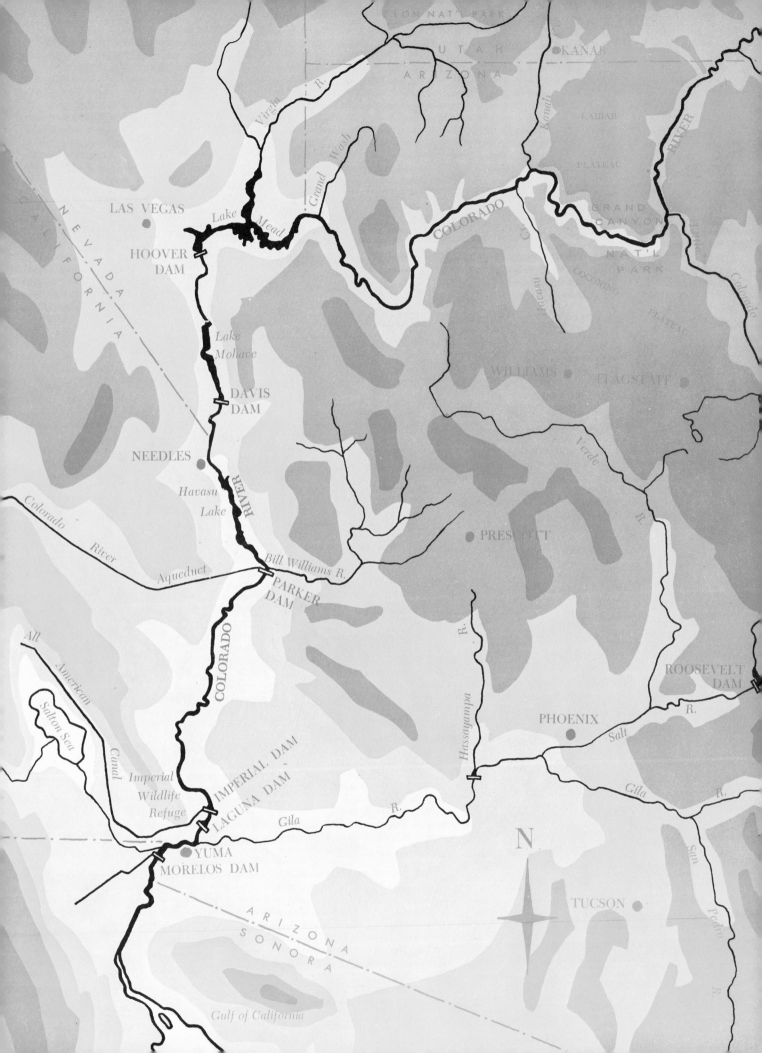

As the brown flood escapes

from the last rapid of Lower Grand Canyon and glides into the narrow head of Lake Mead, it begins to emerge from the land of great blocks. The impassable gorge of vertical walls and steep shelves gradually gives way to broken volcanic terrain. Amid these barren sawtoothed ranges the Colorado descends from one man-made lake to another— driving power generators, bringing bloom to the southern deserts and joy to the hearts of recreationists.

HOOVER DAM

It is fitting that the wild, willful Rio Colorado should be tamed by the highest dam in America and transformed, in passing, into the world's largest artificial lake. Hoover Dam, half again as high as the Washington Monument, impounds at maximum level enough water to cover the state of Connecticut ten feet deep. It was built by six associated companies in the early 1930's to prevent floods and control river flow, to permit irrigation of reclaimed desert lands in Arizona and California, and to generate hydroelectric power. The building of this giant pyramid, with its far-reaching effects and its impact on our national life, culminated a conservation movement officially begun in 1922 with the Colorado River Compact, which apportioned the water

Dams, Dusty Water & Green Paradise

169

between the Upper (Wyoming, Colorado, Utah, New Mexico) and Lower (Nevada, Arizona, California) Basins. While this regional groundwork was being laid, Congress was under pressure for protection of Imperial Valley by an upstream dam and a new canal wholly on American soil to bypass the problem of unregulated Mexican water withdrawal. A huge public campaign, official river surveys, and a violent power controversy led ultimately to the 1928 passage of the Boulder Canyon Act by the United States Congress. This by no means ended the struggle, for the apportionment of power and water among the states had yet to be established. Preliminary agreement on these phases was achieved in 1930, and the Colorado River Project was launched, at a total cost of $400,000,000.

LAKE MEAD

Construction of the dam was completed in 1935, the reservoir began to fill, and the closure of a golden key started power flowing to the Pacific Coast. Lake Mead has impounded Colorado River waters for 115 miles and has made accessible to the sightseer many of our country's wildest and most beautiful desert canyons, some virtually unvisited by man before the lake was formed. The inevitable silt deposit is very evident along upstream shorelines. This unusual lake is set, not among green forested slopes and sunwashed beaches, but in the midst of a stark confusion of jagged peaks, eroded mesas, old lava flows, and weird granite outcrops, grotesquely ornamented with joshua trees and cholla cactus. It reaches far back into the washes and side canyons of the river's tributaries—the Virgin, Meadow Valley Wash, Grand Wash, and others—and its still blue depths have penetrated several miles of the little-known lower Grand Canyon. In these depths lie the remains of three human communities which lived a thousand years apart—the small Mormon towns of Callville and St. Thomas, and the Pueblo Grande de Nevada, a prehistoric Indian village.

VIRGIN RIVER AND ZION CANYON

Dwarfed by the grandeur of the lake which absorbs it, the Virgin River is nonetheless a notable stream. Its two branches rise on the slopes of the Markagunt Plateau, one of the high plateaus which face the Colorado River in southern Utah. The East Fork is formed by the gathering of small streams which drain the eastern margins of the Markagunt. These rivulets join in a valley which follows the Sevier fault and flow south, then west, across the face of the White Cliffs to meet the North Fork of the Virgin. The latter stream has cut a trench through more than 2,000 feet of rock which forms the White and Vermillion Cliffs, to fashion one of the matchless wonders of the West—Zion Canyon. This spectacular defile with its towering red-and-white walls is the combined result of rushing stream water, ground seepage, and other erosive forces upon the soft shales and sandstones which compose the cliffs. The Virgin River, which flows today in approximately the same course as before the canyon was formed, is the chief agent in its evolution. Rapid downcutting in the weakly cemented sandstones, accelerated by regional uplift, has enabled the stream to excavate a narrow, deep canyon with sheer monolithic walls. Widening of the canyon has been accomplished by undercutting action of ground seeps, springs, and the river itself; this results in upward fracture of the cliffs, so that great slabs and fragments fall to the canyon floor, where they quickly disintegrate.

From the junction of its two forks at the boundary of Zion National Park, the Virgin courses through a number of cultivated valleys where nearly all of its flow is diverted for irrigation. A

Dams,
Dusty Water &
Green Paradise

171

chain of small towns has grown up in these valleys; most of them were settled by Mormons who came to southern Utah in the middle years of the last century. Finally, at the end of its long traverse, the muddy little river merges into the north fork of Lake Mead a few miles west of the Nevada-Arizona border, thus joining the Colorado in a far different way from the pattern ordained by Nature.

RIVER TRAVELERS

Two early Colorado voyages in this region have become part of the river's lore through published reports. In the winter of 1837 the trapper Antoine Leroux set out downstream from the mouth of the Virgin River by skin canoe, trapping as he went. As soon as he found timber about forty miles below the Virgin, he built the first of a series of wooden canoes with which he traveled the full length of the Lower Colorado until he reached tidewater. In this distance of about 400 miles he reported, "nothing that I know could stop a small steamboat . . . (except that there may be some hidden rocks under the water that cannot be seen)." With qualifications, this was true, although commercial steamboating which developed in later years seldom ascended the Colorado more than half that distance.

The other, more controversial, Colorado River traveler was James White, a simple prospector whose claim of having passed through the Grand Canyon by raft in 1867 gave rise to much speculation. Robert B. Stanton in his "Colorado River Controversies" stated that after intensive research he had concluded this man actually floated down about sixty miles of the river from a point near the mouth of Grand Wash—many miles below even the Lower Granite Gorge—to the now-flooded town of Callville, Nevada, where he was taken from his raft dazed, starved, and suffering

172

from extreme exposure. Major Powell interviewed White before his own Colorado voyage and felt the story could not be credited, at least in regard to the Grand Canyon. Even today, however, river historians can be found who believe White rafted down through the lower Glen, Marble, and Grand Canyons in fourteen days, as he claimed.

Lake Mead and Davis Dam

From the sluiceways of Hoover Dam the Colorado issues, altered in quality and quantity, but by no means in design. It continues its course southward through a region of gigantic faults, where the elevated blocks form mountains and the lowered ones form valleys now partially filled with alluvium. As would be expected, the storage and power dams are located where the river flows through mountain ranges, allowing the steep canyon walls to be used as abutments for the structure.

Below Hoover Dam is another reservoir, Lake Mohave, which occupies Black and Pyramid Canyons and which is part of the Lake Mead Recreation Area. The clear green waters of Mohave are impounded by Davis Dam, an intermediate regulating structure build in 1946-1951 under provisions of the United States-Mexico water treaty. This princely example of hydroelectric engineering, together with the diversion works at the international boundary, delivers 1,500,000 acre-feet of water each year to the Mexican canal system. It also has a generating capacity of 225,000 horsepower, which is allocated to Nevada, Arizona and California.

In the early 1860's a party of emigrants nearing the Colorado River on Beale's new wagon road was ambushed by Mohave Indians. In the military engagement which followed, the Mohaves were decisively beaten by U.S. troops, and Fort Mohave was es-

Dams,
Dusty Water &
Green Paradise

173

tablished on the banks of the Colorado opposite present Needles, California. The Fort became a principal river port during the steamboating era, with a ferry to exchange supplies from Needles for gold ore produced by Arizona mines around Oatman. A few miles below the old fort, now part of an Indian reservation, the Colorado today is bridged by continental highway, railroad, and a major gas pipeline at Topock, Arizona.

HAVASU LAKE AND THE PARKER PROJECT; BILL WILLIAMS RIVER

Thirty-five miles below Davis Dam begins still another long, narrow reservoir known as Havasu Lake, whose waters are impounded by Parker Dam. Parker was built to supply domestic water via 242 miles of aqueduct to the Metropolitan Water District at Los Angeles, which agency financed the dam's construction. It also controls flood water from the Williams River and generates 120,000 horsepower of electric energy which is consolidated with the output from Davis power plant in a single system. Havasu Lake is 46 miles long and affords fishing, boating, and other recreational facilities, as do Mohave and Mead. Bass, catfish, crappie, and numerous other species are taken in all these lakes, but only Mead and Mohave waters are cold enough to support trout. A national wildlife refuge has been established on Havasu from the dam to the city of Needles.

As an interesting sidelight of the main Colorado River development problem, the Parker project caused a violent inter-state contest, since it implied that California would receive not only the lion's share of power from Hoover Dam, but 5,500,000 of the 7,500,000 acre-feet of water apportioned to the Lower Basin states. Arizona loaded her state militia on a small steamboat and dispatched them upstream to the town of Parker, where they remained at anchor, interrupting work on the dam for several months,

174

until the Metropolitan Water District agreed to modify its demands for the time being. The dam and aqueduct finally became a reality in 1938, though Arizona did not ratify the Colorado River Compact until 1944. Indeed, the Colorado feud is not yet ended. Negotiation over boundaries and apportionment of water and power continues among the Basin states, as well as the important problem of development of public lands in the river bottoms.

Bill Williams River, which empties into Havasu Lake just above the dam, is a short steep tributary whose sources are in the desert ranges southwest of Prescott. The river was named for a fantastic figure of Western frontier history—old Bill Williams. Mountaineer, trapper and scout, he was a shaggy, solitary man who had more the ways of an Indian than of a white. Acknowledged one of the best guides in the early West, he was unjustly blamed for the tragic failure of John Fremont's fourth expedition in the San Juan Mountains during the winter of 1848-49. The Williams River, like most desert streams, is subject to flash-flooding, an important factor in the location of Parker Dam. The Alamo Dam is to be built by the Army Corps of Engineers on this small river for flood control and eventually to make use of the water which is so precious a commodity in this region of perennial drought.

Parker Dam is linked with the town of Parker by a scenic loop highway which is the site of intensive resort development along both shores of the Colorado. A few miles above the town is Headgate Rock Dam, locally known as the "Squaw," which diverts water for agriculture and domestic use to the Colorado River Indian Reservation. Here 40,000 acres of bottomland farms produce a multi-million-dollar crop of cotton, melons, grain and feed crops.

Dams,
Dusty Water &
Green Paradise

175

From Parker to Mexico the river flows with an average drop of 1.4 feet to the mile; its flood plain is generally several miles wide, with adjoining benchlands elevated only a few hundred feet. Though a handful of white men's communities have grown up along the Colorado in the 200 miles between Needles and Yuma, until the present era of mass recreation most of this desert land was sparsely populated by Indian tribes. Evidence of several ethnologic periods of these people has been found and given careful study by archaeologists. A number of unique artifacts have been discovered in recent years by observant airmen near the river, above and below Parker Dam. These huge primitive figures chiefly of humans and animals, were scraped and treaded into the brown gravel of the desert. The longest of the figures measure 160 to 170 feet. They are believed be be effigies made by the Yuma Indians between the sixteenth and mid-nineteenth centuries, and to be related to an ancient Yuma-Pima lengend of a half-human female monster and "Big Brother", her slayer.

Torrent in the Desert

In the general vicinity of the effigies are the vanishing ruins of two Arizona ghost towns, Ehrenburg and LaPaz, placer mining camps of the 1860's. These differed from other defunct mining centers in that they also served as shipping points on a passenger-freight route which involved the use of ocean-going vessels up the Gulf of California, transfer to shallow-draft river steamers which plied the Colorado, and final trans-shipment via wagon train to inland Arizona communities. This river traffic was maintained from about 1852, when Captain Turnbull first transported army supplies in a side-wheeler from Puerto Ysabel to Fort Yuma, until completion of the Southern Pacific Railroad in 1878, which linked the Fort with the west coast.

Early steamboating on the Colorado had some ludicrous phases because of inadequate knowledge of the river's hazards. Submerged sandbars and rocks, unpredictable tides and currents in a stream that was more soil than water thwarted the plans of several would-be navigators. The most publicized of these was Lieutenant Joseph Christmas Ives. Under War Department auspices a specially designed steel steamboat named "Explorer" was built in Philadelphia and shipped in pieces around Cape Horn to the head of the Gulf of California. There is was reassembled under the most harrassing difficulties and finally floated under Ives' command in December 1857. After nearly capsizing in a moderate sea and becoming grounded many times in the sandbar-ridden channel, the Explorer was at last able to move upstream a little slower than a man could walk, accompanied by a group of hilariously amused Indians who followed her along the shore. Near the present site of Hoover Dam she struck a sunken boulder and suffered such grave injury that Ives abandoned ship, continued his tour by skiff and by land. The Ives party visited Grand Canyon (the first known whites to set foot in its bottom) and the Hopi pueblos before returning to Yuma. The topographer of this safari, Egloffstein, stumbled into Havasupai canyon while searching for water—the first European visitor to reach this spot since Father Garces.

Of the Hualpai and Coconino Plateau country at the Grand Canyon's south rim Ives wrote, "The region last explored is, of course, absolutely valueless. It can be approached only from the south, and after entering it there is nothing to do but leave. Ours was the first and doubtless will be the last party of whites to visit this profitless locality. It seems intended by nature that the Colorado River along the greater portion of its lone and majestic

Dams, Dusty Water & Green Paradise

177

way shall be forever unvisited and unmolested." It appears that the Lieutenant was not clairvoyant in this respect, though he displayed unusual talent in the art of description. His eloquent report of the Lower Colorado canyons stands as a literary masterpiece.

Imperial Dam

The Colorado and its desert environs present a rather monotonous appearance between the Parker valley and the beginning of the Imperial reservoir, except for the new Palo Verde Dam, which diverts water to a large irrigation project in the Palo Verde country of California. There is little about this ribbon of clear blue-green water, moving almost imperceptibly among the gray dunes and low volcanic ridges, to suggest its dramatic upstream career or the influential role it has played in human affairs. Eighteen miles above Yuma the river is impounded by Imperial Dam to form a long winding lake. As in the case of other Lower Colorado reservoirs, fishing resorts and trailer camps have been developed at several access points. Here also a national wildlife refuge has been established. Imperial waters are diverted to the All-American Canal for irrigation in Salton Basin, a part of the Colorado-Gila delta region, and to the Gravity-Main Canal for the Gila Project in Arizona. The dam is a 45-foot diversion weir about two-thirds of a mile long. Behind this rather modest structure lies an incredible story of natural forces and man's age-old struggle to control them.

In past millennia the northern tip of the Gulf of California was gradually sealed off from the main body of water by a geologic mechanism which has not yet been ascertained. The massive sediment deposits in this region apparently were derived from both the Gila and the Colorado. These deposits may have been solely responsible for the damming, but it is also possible

178

that a deformation of the earth's crust played a dominant role. Whatever the cause, a sink resulted which is structurally continuous with the Gulf, entirely below sea level, and now partially occupied by a "sea" whose only outlet is by evaporation.

The most extraordinary meander of the Colorado River in historic times occurred in 1905-07, when an unusual series of floods carried river water over the low barrier which separated the modern channel from Salton Basin. The unforeseen volume of flood water washed out the inlet dam of a diversion channel constructed by the California Development Company to provide irrigation water for Imperial Valley, widened the artificial opening in the river banks, and destroyed successive efforts to seal the intake until February 1907, when the break was finally closed. During this two-year period great canyons were eroded in the soft valley floor; large tracts of settled and irrigated land were inundated; the Basin was carpeted with a silt deposit equal to four times the volume of the Panama Canal excavation; Salton Sea was formed by the overflow; and the Southern Pacific Railroad was compelled to relocate its main line on higher ground. The railroad also was obliged, in default of support by the irrigation company and the federal government, to underwrite the heroic efforts to halt the flood, at a cost of three million dollars. As a happier aftermath to this gargantuan destruction, the rich soil laid down during the flood has facilitated the development of Imperial and Coachella Valleys as centers of fruit and vegetable production on a scale previously unknown; and the catastrophe provided necessary impetus to the development of the present Colorado River regulatory program. Salton Sea still exists as a brackish lake of greatly reduced area; its present sources of water are overflow from the irrigation canals and underground drainage from nearby mountains. The Colorado, now securely

Dams,
Dusty Water &
Green Paradise

179

contained in its channel under present controls, goes its innocuous way southward.

Four miles downstream from Imperial is the oldest of the Lower Colorado dams—Laguna. Built in 1909, this Indian type diversion weir originally provided irrigation water for a huge reclaimed tract in the desert around Yuma. However, since the completion of Imperial Dam, Laguna serves only to control tailwater from the larger dam.

GILA RIVER

The Gila, which enters the Colorado from the east about seven miles below Laguna, traverses the state of Arizona from east to west, descending from headwaters in the Mogollon range of New Mexico through alternating steep canyons and level valleys flanked by lofty mountain ranges, until it reaches the lower desert. Gila country was not generally known in the States until American troops marched through the river valley in 1847 during the Mexican War. The Gila served as the international boundary until the present line was established by the Gadsden Purchase in 1853. In our times this river and its tributaries are harnessed by a series of storage dams. Though a large volume of water drains from its extensive watershed, the entire flow is diverted for irrigation and other uses; Painted Rock Dam leaves the Gila essentially a dry bed for 126 miles from its mouth.

HISTORIC YUMA

The city of Yuma, now the shipping center for a vast irrigated produce area in southwestern Arizona, owes its origin to a natural crossing of the Colorado River near the Gila's mouth. Following its discovery by Jesuits in 1539, this convenient crossing was used by the missionaries, soldiers, and colonists who passed down the

180

Gila Valley on their way to California coastal settlements. In 1849 a ferry was established to accommodate the flood of emigrants during the California gold rush. As the story goes, a traveling party of U.S. engineers found the ferryman's rates so excessive that they decided to lay out a town and offer him a building lot in exchange for passage. The plan succeeded and the town later came into existence. Twice renamed, Yuma has prospered variously as a gold-mining town, river shipping port, territorial honky-tonk, county seat, and now a busy commercial and tourist center. Arizona's first territorial prison was carved into a bluff of solid granite which overlooks the Colorado here.

THE LAST HUNDRED MILES

A short distance below the Gila's mouth the diminished Colorado turns sharply west, passing north of Yuma, then continues southward. Near this point in the year 1701 Father Eusebio Kino was towed across the river on a raft by Quiquima Indians for a gala visit to their homeland. Though he was unable to fulfill his ambition of blazing a trail to the Pacific Coast, this tireless Jesuit did explore the Gila River and map accurately the upper Gulf of California. At the U.S.-Mexico boundary Colorado water is diverted for the last time by Morelos Dam, built in compliance with the international treaty to supply users south of the border. Here the stream flows languidly toward the Gulf on a bed that has been elevated 100 to 300 feet above the mean level of the region by past deposition of silt from its own stream and that of the Gila. Along its banks, extending as far southward as cultivation is possible, are citrus groves, produce ranches, and huge cotton plantations, all sustained by Colorado River water. Since completion of the high storage dams, the main silt burden formerly carried to the ocean settles out in reservoirs; and great vol-

Dams,
Dusty Water &
Green Paradise

181

umes of water are withdrawn for irrigation and domestic use, so that the building-up process and danger of flooding have been checked. The water here is now a clear, limpid green, probably for the first time since the Colorado watershed achieved continental status. In its final eighty miles the attenuated river wanders among the aggregation of mud flats, dry lakes and salt marshes which compose its present delta. It still varies considerably in volume and appearance due to the law of supply and demand.

Below tidewater, geysers, fresh-water upwellings, and lagoons of high mineral content evidence the unsettled nature of the underlying crust. Great chunks of the silt block occasionally slide off into deeper waters of the Gulf, causing violent local marine disturbances. Another phenomenon of the Colorado, known as the "bore," used to occur in greatly exaggerated form on collision of the muddy river current with rising tides in the narrow Gulf before the river was so greatly reduced by upstream controls. The "bore" was a monumental wall of water which developed during high tides, moving upstream over the river current; such waves have been known to reach a height near forty feet. The tidal crests were the cause of great apprehension and danger to early navigators of the lower channel. Today the river exerts no considerable influence upon tidal activity, but high tides continue to build as they approach the narrow head of the Gulf of California and enter the estuary. At last, its long adventure completed and its ageless story written in the sands of time, a trailing remnant of the mighty Colorado merges with the blue oceanic waters of the Gulf.

EARLY CONQUEST OF THE LOWER BASIN

The earliest recorded history of the Rio Colorado pertains to its delta, an incidental finding in the search for an easy route

182

to the Seven Cities of Cibola. These Zuñi pueblos, which in reality differed little from other sixteen-century Indian adobe villages, had become the subject of fantastic legends of wealth. When these reports reached the Spanish conquistadores in Mexico, plundering expeditions were soon organized with Cibola as their objective.

In 1539 Hernando Cortez, who had already taken incalculable riches in the land of the Aztecs, outfitted three ships under command of Francisco de Ulloa to sail northward along the west coast of Mexico to the latitude of Cibola; from there his troops were to march overland for the conquest. This, of course, he did not accomplish. He sailed his ships up the Gulf of California to the actual mouth of the Colorado, where he witnessed the phenomenon of the tidal bore and decided not to court disaster by proceeding further. For this reason Ulloa cannot be considered the discoverer of the Colorado River. He wrote, ". . . it seemed there was an inlet in the mouths of certain lakes whereby the sea went in and out. There were divers opinions amongst us and some thought that the current entered into these lakes, and also that some great river might be the cause thereof . . ." Though he returned to Mexico empty-handed, this would-be plunderer did ascertain that Baja California was not an island, as supposed, but a peninsula.

The persistent myth of Cibola continued to attract other gold-seekers on the grand scale. In the year after Ulloa's voyage Francisco de Coronado, a provisional governor of Mexico, led the cavalry division of a vast two-armed expedition, and Hernando de Alarcon sailed his three ships north from San Miguel on the Mexican coast, with orders to intercept Coronado's forces nearer the scene of conquest and deliver supplies to them. The existence and location of the Colorado River were, of course, unknown at that time. Alarcon succeeded in entering the river's

Dams,
Dusty Water &
Green Paradise

183

mouth despite the 3-foot tides of that season and achieved the first European penetration of the Colorado. His ships passed through the estuary with great difficulty; then, "it pleased God that after this sort we came to the very bottom of the bay, where we found a very mighty river, which ran with so great fury of a storm that we could hardly sail against it." Some friendly Cocopah Indians were persuaded to hand-tow the ships to the mouth of the Gila, and the expedition subsequently moved a hundred miles farther upstream in an effort to establish contact with the land forces. Failing in this, the commander turned about and sailed for home. Melchior Diaz, the Coronado liaison officer sometimes credited with discovery of the Colorado, actually reached the river rendezvous some weeks after Alarcon's departure. Meanwhile, Coronado had arrived at Cibola, exposed the empty legend, and avenged his disappointment upon the simple pueblos and their occupants, ending forever the dream of grand Spanish conquest in the Colorado River Basin.

NINETEENTH CENTURY EXPLORATION

During the 280 years that followed Alarcon's voyage there was no further recorded up-river penetration of the delta by white men, though it was briefly visited by land expeditions of Oñate and Anza, as well as by Jesuit and Franciscan missionaries who brought Christianity to the Indian tribes of the Southwest. In 1826—the year of James Pattie's pedestrian invasion of the Colorado—a young British naval lieutenant, R. W. H. Hardy, sailed a small schooner up the Gulf of California to investigate the Gulf's old pearl fisheries for a London syndicate. Following Hardy's visit the next reconnaissance of the river was occasioned by the need for an alternative supply route between the Pacific coast and Fort Yuma, which had been established on the Colorado River for pro-

184

tection of the 1849 gold-seekers. Lieutenant George H. Derby, a War Department topographer, was unable to sail his clumsy transport ship beyond the tidewater shoals where Hardy had gone aground. Derby proceeded upsteram by rowboat, however, and succeeded in gaining enough information for a report to the Secretary of War regarding the type of boat which could navigate the Colorado in all seasons. It is isgnificant that only boats of the design recommended by Derby were found practical during the era of river freighting which followed.

THE DELTA

Though the Colorado was first sighted by white men in the mid-sixteenth century and visited sporadically by them during the next three hundred years, no extensive knowledge of the desert country north of its mouth was gained by the river explorers or by the missionaries and wayfarers who came after them. The first valid reconnaissance of the delta and adjoining lands was incidental to the 1849 gold rush to California, with the development of overland trails and stage routes from Yuma to the coast. Completion of the southern Pacific Railroad in 1879 removed the last obstacle to east-west travel, and by 1905 Imperial Valley numbered its inhabitants at 12,000. Today, after half a century of progress, the delta country affords livelihood for 75,000 residents of the Basin and enriches the table of countless millions who enjoy the year-round flow of crisp vegetables and sun-ripened fruit.

PERPETUAL TRANSFORMATION

Thus it appears that in our times the Colorado ends its impetuous and destructive career in a reversal—the building of useful soil bodies and the provision of life-giving moisture in an empty land. Its natural history is based on elements common to all rivers

185

which flow to the sea: a primary response to the pull of gravity in finding the lowest channel; adaptation to externally imposed changes as well as those wrought by its own activity; and gradual wearing away of the entire region drained by the river until a mean level is reached. In the case of the Colorado these processes have been more accelerated and dramatic than of other American rivers, for example those with watersheds that are gently sloping and clothed with vegetation. Because it courses a region preponderantly desert, the Colorado has funneled a great flood of alluvium which readily parts from the barren slopes of its basin. The suspended particles continue to move as long as the stream flows, settling to the bed when they reach slack water. Thus we find silt accumulation at the heads of reservoirs and normally in the tidewater zone, where it constantly builds seaward.

Because of the peculiar structural and behavioral qualities of the Colorado, its tremendous delta has been transformed by the inspired labor of man into the most productive of all America's river deltas. The rich soil laid down by the River in past ages feeds the great orchards and truck gardens of the Arizona and California deserts, while today's Colorado supplies water to the canal systems which sustain their fruitful development.

The process which began with a tiny rivulet of snow water and a grain of sand continues—nations rise and decline; men pass and are forgotten, and their modifications of the River are for a moment in time. Its future is as veiled as the essence of Grand Canyon.

In final analysis, one is compelled to agree with Major Powell and Dr. Widtsoe that "it is useless to describe with words or even with pictures the wonders of surpassing magnitude and beauty" of this great River and the land it has moulded—there remains but to go, to see, to experience!

Angel's Landing Trail,
Zion Canyon

Zion Canyon

The Virgin River

Lake Mead near Pierce's Ferry

Harbor at Lake Mead

Hoover Dam

Willow Beach

Hoover Dam
(facing page)

*Davis Dam and
Lake Mohave*

Pipeline Crossing
at Topock

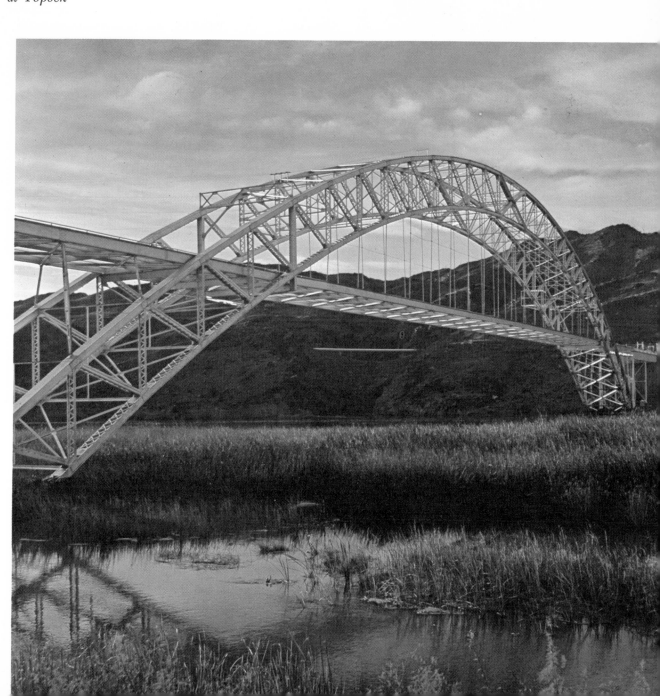

Parker Dam

Near Needles, California

Imperial Dam

*Martinez Lake,
Imperial
Wildlife Refuge*

Imperial Valley

*Romaine Pickers on
the Delta*

*Irrigated Citrus,
Yuma Mesa*

*All American
Canal*

Coolidge Dam on
the Gila River

*Roosevelt Dam on
the Salt River*

*Gates at Morelos Dam,
Mexico
(facing page)*

Truck Farm
near Yuma

The Estuary

Torrent in the Desert

has been designed by John Anderson,
set in Caledonia type, and printed on
Curtis Colophon at Northland Press
Flagstaff, Arizona
Mcmlxii